MEGA

THE COMPLETE REFERENCE
TO DRAWING MANGA

manga

KEITH SPARROW

MEGA

THE COMPLETE REFERENCE
TO DRAWING MANGA

manga

KEITH SPARROW

TANGENT PUBLICATIONS

Published in Canada in 2007
by Tangent Publications
an imprint of
Axis Publishing Limited
8c Accommodation Road
London NW11 8ED
www.axispublishing.co.uk

Creative Director: Siân Keogh
Editorial Director: Anne Yelland
Art Director: Sean Keogh
Designer: Simon de Lotz
Production Manager: Jo Ryan

ISBN 13: 978-1-904707-60-8
ISBN 10: 1-904707-60-2

1 3 5 7 9 10 8 6 4 2

Printed and bound in China

contents

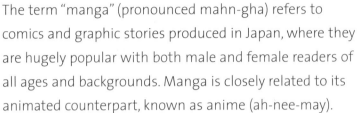

INTRODUCTION

The term "manga" (pronounced mahn-gha) refers to comics and graphic stories produced in Japan, where they are hugely popular with both male and female readers of all ages and backgrounds. Manga is closely related to its animated counterpart, known as anime (ah-nee-may).

Manga stories cover an enormous range of subject matter, with numerous distinct subgenres aimed at different readers, such as *shounen* for boys, and *shoujo* for girls. They sometimes contain images or plotlines that may seem shocking to Western sensibilities, and deal frankly with issues like homosexuality and extreme violence. Stories can also be charmingly romantic and whimsical, however, and ecological and spiritual themes are common. Other popular subjects include science-fiction, horror, sports, and stories featuring traditional Japanese cultural icons like samurai warriors and ninjas.

MANGA IN JAPAN

Manga stories are collected in magazines (*mangashi*), which can be anything from around 200 pages long to 1000-page volumes as thick as telephone directories, and are sold at low prices in vast quantities, with color usually limited to the cover and a few selected pages inside. Because of their size, it's not practical for the average person to collect the *mangashi*, so they are often left lying around in public places, where a passer-by can pick them up and read. A typical *mangashi* may contain several ongoing serials, and these serials are often collected into a separate compact volume (*tankobon*), which we are more familiar with in Western bookshops.

ORIGINS OF THE STYLE

The distinctive visual characteristics of modern manga, as we know it, can be traced back to Osamu Tezuka, and his groundbreaking series, *Tetsuwan Atom* (*Astro Boy*) in 1951. Born in the shadow of then-recent developments in nuclear power, *Astro Boy* was an endearingly cute robot character, who caught the public imagination to such an extent that the series eventually ran for 17 years. The artwork in *Astro Boy* introduced many of the characteristics we now associate with manga, including the large eyes and spiky hair. Tezuka was a prolific artist

and writer, creating many outstanding manga tales, including the first significant *shoujo*, or girls' manga, with *Ribon No Kishi* (*Knight in Ribbons*) in 1953.

Tezuka was followed by successive generations of male and female *mangaka* (manga creators) who developed a more gritty, realistic medium for their stories, involving the *yakuza* gangsters of modern Japan, as well as the historical samurai and ninja swordplay of ancient feudal Japan. The violence in some of these stories has led to some criticism in the West, where comics tend to be more restrained, but there is no doubting the popularity of manga combat-based stories among young readers in the USA and Europe, in particular.

THE RISE OF SHOUJO

In 1962, the first steps toward one of today's most popular *shoujo* subgenres were taken, when Fujio Akatsuka created his *Secret Akko-chan*, a story about a young girl given magical powers by a mirror-dwelling spirit. Today, the *mahou* (magical girl) genre is one of the most popular trends in *shoujo* manga, with *Sailor Moon* by Takeuchi Naoko probably the best-known example. *Sailor Moon* is

also an example of another manga subgenre, known as *sentai* (superteam), as the principal character, Tsukino Usagi, was eventually joined by a team of sailor-suited fighters.

CURRENT TRENDS

Another important development in manga was the introduction of giant mechanized battle suits, which eventually led to the giant-robot genre so popular today, such as the *Mobile Suit Gundam* series: to many non-Japanese readers these probably represent the archetypal manga stories. The battle-suit theme was also featured in the immensely successful *Mighty Morphin' Power Rangers* TV series, which prompted many new young readers to seek out manga comics.The popularity of manga and anime has soared in the West, beginning with the US syndication of the more popular anime series in the 1970s. With new soundtracks in English, early mecha and action anime series proved a big hit with American kids. Today, the influence of manga art can be seen around the world, and this book can help you develop some of the basic features and drawing principles which have helped make manga such an inspirational and ground-breaking art-form.

MATERIALS AND EQUIPMENT

You do not need to spend a fortune to get started in drawing and coloring good manga art. You do, however, need to choose your materials with some care to get the best from your work. Start with a few basics and add to your kit as your style develops and you figure out what you like working with.

Artists have their preferences when it comes to equipment, but regardless of personal favorites, you will need a basic set of materials that will enable you to sketch, ink, and color your manga art. The items discussed here are only a guide—don't be afraid to experiment to find out what works best for you.

PAPERS

You will need two types of paper—one for creating sketches, the other for producing finished color artwork.

Graphite pencils are ideal for getting your ideas down on paper, and producing your initial drawing. The pencil drawing is probably the most important stage in creating your artwork. Choose an HB and a 2B to start with.

For quickly jotting down ideas, almost any piece of scrap paper will do. For more developed sketching, though, use tracing paper. Tracing paper provides a smooth surface, helping you to sketch freely. It is also forgiving—any mistakes can easily be erased several times over. Typically, tracing paper comes in pads. Choose a pad that is around 24 lb (90gsm) in weight for best results—lighter tracing papers may buckle and heavier ones are not suitable for sketching.

Once you have finished sketching out ideas, you will need to transfer them to the paper you want to produce your finished colored art on. To do this, you will have to trace over your pencil sketch, so the paper you choose cannot be too opaque or "heavy"—otherwise you will not be able to see the sketch underneath. Choose a paper around 16 lb (60gsm) for this.

The type of paper you use is also important. If you are going to color using marker pens, use "marker" or "layout" paper. Both of these types are very good at holding the ink found in markers. Other papers of the same weight can cause the marker ink to "bleed," that is, the ink soaks beyond the inked lines of your drawing and produces fuzzy edges. This does not look good.

You may wish to color your art using other materials, such as colored pencils or watercolors. "Drawing" paper is good for graphite pencil and inked-only art (such as that found in the majority of manga comic books), while heavyweight watercolor papers hold wet paint and colored inks and come in a variety of surface textures.

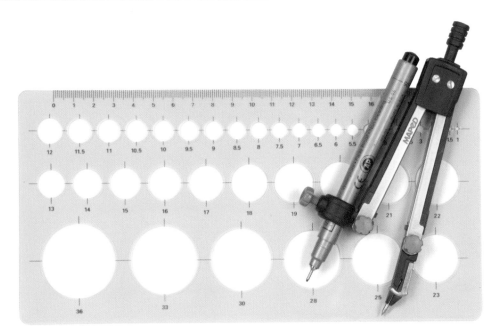

Again, don't be afraid to experiment: you can buy many types of papers in single sheets while you find the ones that suit your artwork best.

PENCILS

The next step is to choose some pencils for your sketches. Pencil sketching is probably the most important stage, and always comes first when producing manga art (you cannot skip ahead to the inking stage), so make sure you choose pencils that feel good in your hand and allow you to express your ideas freely.

Pencils are manufactured in a range of hard and soft leads. Hard leads are designated by the letter H and soft leads by the letter B. Both come in six levels—6H is the hardest lead and 6B is the softest. In the middle is HB, a halfway mark between the two ranges. Generally, an HB and a 2B lead will serve most sketching purposes, with the softer lead being especially useful for loose, "idea" sketches, and the harder for more final lines.

Working freehand allows great freedom of expression and is ideal when you are working out a sketch, but you will find times when precision is necessary.

Use compasses or a circle guide for circles and ellipses to keep your work sharp. Choose compasses that can be adjusted to hold both pencils and pens.

Alternatively, you can opt for mechanical pencils. Also called self-propelling pencils, these come in a variety of lead grades and widths, and never lose their point, making sharpening traditional wood-cased pencils a thing of the past. Whether you use one is entirely up to you—it is possible to get excellent results whichever model you choose.

SHARPENERS AND ERASERS

If you use wooden pencils, you will need to get a quality sharpener; this is a small but essential piece of equipment. Electric sharpeners work very well and are also very fast; they last a long time too. Otherwise, a handheld sharpener is fine. One that comes with a couple of spare blades can be a worthwhile investment, to ensure that your pencils are always sharp.

Along with a sharpener, you will need an eraser for removing any visible pencil lines from your inked sketches prior to coloring. Choose a high-quality eraser that does not smudge the pencil lead, scuff the paper, or leave dirty fragments all over your work. A soft "putty" eraser works best, since it absorbs pencil lead rather than just rubbing it away. For this reason, putty erasers do become dirty with use. Keep yours clean by trimming it carefully with scissors every now and then.

INKING PENS

The range of inking pens can be bewildering, but some basic rules will help you select the pens you need. Inked lines in most types of manga tend to be quite bold so buy a thin-nibbed pen, about 0.5mm and a medium-size nib, about 0.8mm. Make sure that the ink in the pens is waterproof; this won't smudge or run. Next, you will need a medium-tip felt pen. Although you won't need to use this pen very often to ink the outlines of your characters, it is still useful for filling in small detailed areas of solid black. The Pentel sign pen does this job well. Last, consider a pen that can create different line widths according to the amount of pressure you put on the tip. These pens replicate brushes and allow you to create flowing lines such as those seen on hair and clothing. The Pentel brush pen does this very well, delivering a steady supply of ink to the tip from a replaceable cartridge.

Test-drive a few pens at your art store to see which ones suit you best. All pens should produce clean, sharp lines with a deep black pigment.

MARKERS AND COLORING AIDS

Many artists use markers, rather than paint, to color their artwork, because markers are easy to use and come in a huge variety of colors and shades. Good-quality markers, such as those made by Chartpak, Letraset, or Copic, produce excellent, vibrant results, allowing you to build up multiple layers of color so you can create rich, detailed work and precise areas of shading. Make sure that you use your markers with marker or layout paper to avoid bleeding. Markers are often

Felt-tip pens are the ideal way to ink your sketches. A fineliner, medium-tip pen, and sign pen should meet all of your needs, whatever your style and preferred subjects. A few colored felt-tip pens can be a good addition to your kit, allowing you to introduce color at the inking stage.

Markers come in a wide variety of colors, which allows you to achieve subtle variations in tone. In addition to a thick nib for broad areas of color, the Copic markers shown here feature a thin nib for fine detail.

refillable, so they last a long time. The downside is that they are expensive, so choose a limited number of colors to start with, and add as your needs evolve. As always, test out a few markers in your art store before buying any.

However, markers are not the only coloring media. Paints and gouache also produce excellent results, and can give your work a distinctive look. Add white gouache, which comes in a tube, to your work to create highlights and sparkles of light. Apply it in small quantities with a good-quality watercolor brush.

It is also possible to color your artwork on computer. This is quick to do, although obviously there is a high initial outlay. It also tends to produce flatter color than markers or paints.

DRAWING AIDS

Most of your sketching will be done freehand, but there are situations, especially with man-made objects such as the edges of buildings or the wheels of a car, when your line work needs to be crisp and sharp to create the right look. Rulers, circle guides, and compasses all provide this accuracy. Rulers are either metal or plastic; in most cases, plastic ones work best, though metal ones tend to last longer. For circles, use a circle guide, which is a plastic sheet with a wide variety of different-sized holes stamped out of it. If the circle you want to draw is too big for the circle guide, use a compass that can hold a pencil and inking pen.

A selection of warm and cool grays is a useful addition to your marker colors and most ranges feature several different shades. These are ideal for shading on faces, hair, and clothes.

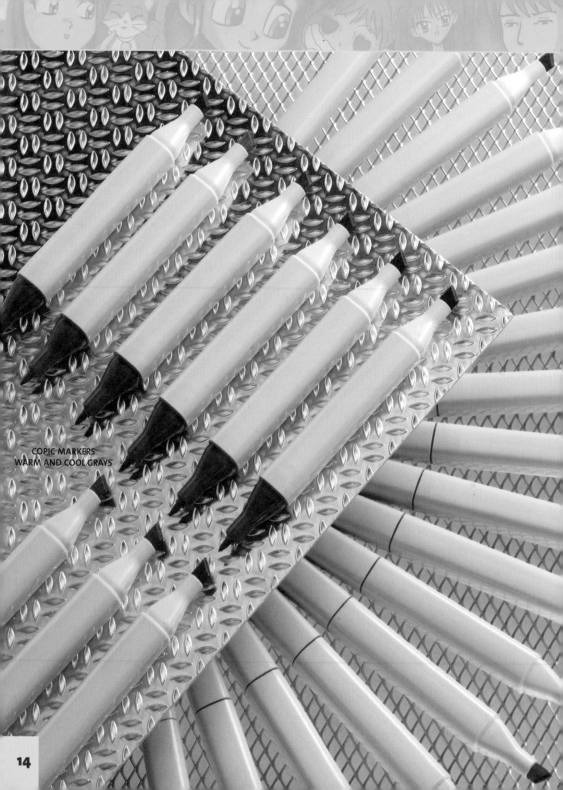

COPIC MARKERS
WARM AND COOL GRAYS

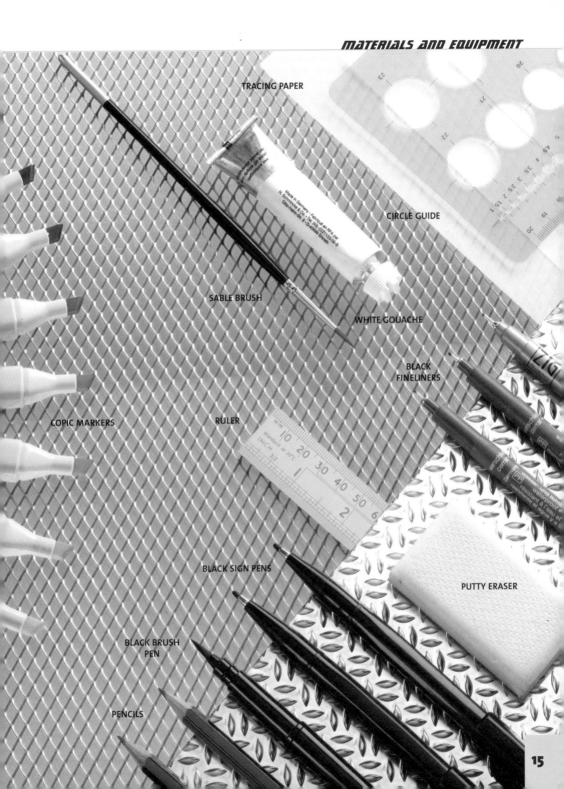

TRACING PAPER

CIRCLE GUIDE

SABLE BRUSH

WHITE GOUACHE

BLACK FINELINERS

COPIC MARKERS

RULER

BLACK SIGN PENS

PUTTY ERASER

BLACK BRUSH PEN

PENCILS

Figures

You will need to be able to draw a variety of figures to people your manga story. This chapter shows you the basics of manga anatomy through drawing a series of male and female figures from all angles, and in a variety of poses. Here, the figures are more important than what they are wearing or their individual faces and hairstyles.

THREE-QUARTER VIEW

A basic sense of anatomy and proportion is essential when drawing manga. Here we have a basic female manga character in a relaxed three-quarter-angle pose, with hand on hip, and wearing a simple school-uniform consisting of a blouse, tank-top, skirt, and long socks. The outfit should be secondary to the figure itself, and added after the basic body is constructed.

Now flesh out the body. Draw curved lines down to a trim waist, then arms, with her left hand on her hip. Draw her legs and splayed feet, then indicate breasts.

Give her bangs and a spiky ponytail, then add school-uniform style clothes. Note how the sleeves and skirt spread out from the body and indicate where the tank-top creases at the waist.

Sketch a balloon shape for her head, tapering to a point for her chin. Use a series of lines and ovals to indicate her limbs and joints. A female is about six heads high.

Add manga-style facial features, such as large eyes, tiny nose, and a small, smiling mouth, and her visible left ear. Refine the lines of her left arm and, especially, her left hand.

BACK VIEW

Try to think of your character as a three-dimensional person, one that you can draw from any angle. To help you with this, take the previous character and draw a back view of her standing. Figure out how low her ponytail falls, and where her various joints and clothes line up. Her body will be roughly symmetrical.

Flesh out the torso, tapering into a tiny waist, then out again over the hips to the line of the skirt. Then draw down the outsides of her legs.

Sketch flowing lines over the head and down her back for hair. Finally add clothing details: the ribbing on the tank, and at the top of the socks, and the short sleeves of her shirt.

Draw a center line, then add a balloon shape for the head. Draw vertical lines for the arms and legs, and horizontals for the shoulders and waist. Use ovals for the joints, and triangles for the feet.

Add a neck and shoulder blades, then flesh out the arms and draw in hands. Then draw the insides of the legs, so that you have created two separate legs.

PROFILE VIEW

Continuing with the same pose, try and draw your figure from the side, or profile view. In contrast to the rear view, the profile is not symmetrical, and it's important to understand how the contours of the body line up.

Add a circle for the shoulder joint and an oval for the pelvis. Join the head and pelvis at the back and front, creating the curve of the breast. Then add the leg and foot.

Finally add the clothing details. From this angle, the collar is visible, the sleeve tapers out, and there is a little ribbing around the tank armhole and neck. Add the skirt, sock, and shoe.

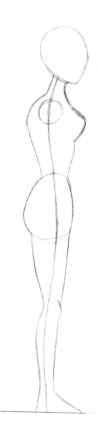

Draw an egg shape for the head, with its point for the chin. The spine is essentially an elongated S-shape and the legs are curved. Draw a horizontal for the floor.

Refine the profile of the face, giving the figure a small nose, then add an eye and eyebrow, the mouth, and a C for the ear. Draw hair on the head and sketch the lines of the ponytail, then add tapering lines for the arm and create the individual fingers.

VIEW FROM ABOVE

Drawing views from above involves foreshortening, which is a way of showing how the eye interprets distances in unusual perspectives. Here, the torso will be dramatically shorter than usual, and the feet will be smaller to indicate the distance from the eye. The character is looking up at the viewer so the face will be clearly visible. This makes the pose more dramatic.

Draw an egg shape with the chin facing off to one side. Use an ellipse and triangle for the pelvis, lines for the legs and arms, and a circle for the shoulder joint.

Start to flesh out the body by adding a torso. Then draw in the arms, with elbows and hands. Complete this stage by drawing the legs, with knee joints, and feet.

Note that there is no neck visible from this angle. Now add facial features: large manga eyes, eyebrows, a tiny nose, and a mouth. Add hair and fingers.

Start to add clothing details: the collar and sleeves of the shirt, the ribbing on the tank and socks, and the skirt. Add her shoes last.

This time go to the next stage and ink your drawing. Choose the most important lines to ink, and work carefully on top of the pencil marks. You can use solid black in some areas to give your drawing more impact, such as the shadow under the chin, and her shoes. Add some fine lines to indicate creases and folds in the clothing.

KNEELING, LEANING FORWARD

Drawing a figure with bended arms or legs can present a new challenge. This character is kneeling down and leaning toward the viewer. Her weight is supported by her outstretched arms and she is looking attentively with a slightly tilted head.

Draw an egg head, a curving line for the back and ovals for the buttocks and thighs. Draw a curving horizontal out to the shoulders, and ines for the arms.

Add the neck and shoulders, then give her a torso with fairly large breasts. Next give her arms, with hands on the floor, then flesh out her legs, and add a foot.

Put in the facial features of large eyes with eyebrows, tiny nose, and mouth. Add long flowing hair, then start to block out the darkest areas of the drawing.

When the ink is dry, erase the pencil lines. Color her skin pale pink, then give her some red hair, leaving a white highlight on each side. Finally use a mid blue for the areas of detail on the swimsuit.

Ink all the main lines of the drawing. Then ink the area of neck where the collar sits, and the swimsuit. Leave some areas white to add color detail later.

STANDING WITH ATTITUDE

As a graphic story-telling medium, manga relies heavily on body language to convey the personality and moods of its characters. This manga girl is standing with her arms folded and her weight on her back leg, with an arched back and slightly inclined head, giving her a sulky, confrontational look.

Draw an egg-shaped head, then a center line. Bisect this and add circles for shoulder joints and lines for arms. Add a triangle for the pelvis and stick legs and feet.

Flesh out the arms and add a torso by joining the arms and pelvis. Draw circles for the hip joints, then draw in the legs. Add in large ellipses for the feet.

She is looking away to her left so give her pupils looking in this direction. Add eyebrows, nose, and mouth, then give her some shaggy cropped hair.

Now work on the details of the clothing. She is wearing a fitted cropped top with a collar, tight jeans with a belt, and large futuristic boots.

Ink the main lines, then use solid black for the shadow on the neck. Ink in the cuff of a glove, then use a fineliner to indicate folds in the clothing.

SITTING PRETTY

A sitting posture is an interesting challenge to a manga artist. Here is a girl in a demure long dress, sitting attentively on a large footstool. Her hands are clasped between her knees and her back is arched up, giving her an innocent air.

Draw an egg head and a curving center line, then bisect the line with a horizontal. Add circles for the shoulder joints and lines for the arms. Draw an ellipse for the pelvis and circles for the knees.

Join the head and shoulders, and flesh out the arms. Give her a torso and breasts. Add flesh to the top of her left leg by joining the hip and knee joints. Add both lower legs and the pointed feet.

Now start to get some detail into her face and clothing. Add large eyes, a tiny nose, and a smiling mouth. Give her shoulder-length straight hair and spiky bangs. She is wearing a fitted demure dress and ballet pumps.

Ink all the main lines of her face, figure, and clothing, then ink around the footstool, and block out the shadow areas on her legs and on the stool legs. Color her hair, leaving white highlights on the crown and on each side of her head.

Use the signpen to color the pumps. Then color her face, neck, the bit of visible hand, and her legs pale pink. Use darker pink to create the shadow cast by her hair on her face and neck. Finally use a bright red to color her dress.

RUNNING FAST

In this pose the straight leading leg is showing the speed of the girl's movement, and there is a slight foreshortening on the trailing leg. Note in a running stance how the arms and legs operate on opposite sides, so if the left leg is forward then the right arm is also forward, and vice versa.

Draw a balloon-shaped head with pointed chin. Add a center line. Use circles for the shoulders, elbow, hips, and knees, and join with lines for the legs and arms. Add simple fists.

Flesh out the body. Add a neck, work along the arms and fists, then down the torso. Indicate her breasts. Work down the nearest leg, adding a running shoe, then flesh out the back leg and shoe.

Give her eyes, a nose, a mouth, and one ear. Add spiky bangs and tied-back hair. Create the teeshirt and shorts, add socks, and refine the shoes.

Work around the figure, inking the main lines of the head, body, clothing, and shoes. Use the inking pen to add folds in the clothing and socks. When the ink is dry, erase any pencil lines.

Color her skin pale pink, and blend in red-brown shadows. Give her bright blue hair, with darker blue shadows. Add blue-gray for the teeshirt. Finally, color the shoes pink.

RUNNING LEAP

Here, a tough-looking action girl in a futuristic jumpsuit leaps into view. Her long flowing hair trails behind, giving a useful emphasis to her movement. Her left leg is bent tightly forward at the knee, suggesting she has just used this leg to push off from a point behind. The body is tightly compacted for flight, except for the right leg, which is stretched out ready for a landing.

Create an egg-shaped head with pointed chin, then use a curved line for the spine. Use circles for the shoulder joints, elbow, and knees, and a large circle for the hip. Add straight lines for the bent arm and both the legs.

Add some detail to the body. Add the neck and flesh out the torso. Add the arms and legs, making the top of the leg closest to you fairly muscular. Draw in simply shaped hands and feet.

Next work on the facial details, giving her large expressive eyes with arched eyebrows, and a small nose and mouth. Use a few simple lines to create her hair which is streaming out behind her.

Ink all the main lines of your composition. Then use the fineliner to indicate some folds in the clothing around the elbow and knees. When the ink is dry, carefully erase any pencil lines you no longer need.

Start to add some detail to her clothing, then use your pencil to create areas of shading on her top and cuffs, and on the flashes on her pants. Give her pumping fists and shade these too.

OVER THE SHOULDER

A good understanding of the figure from all sides will be useful when tackling an unusual pose like this. A beautiful but tough-looking girl looks back over her shoulder toward you. Her weight is balanced evenly and her knees are slightly bent in case a fast movement is necessary. The forward tilt of the head indicates a guarded curiosity, as if she's heard a noise behind her that might be a threat. Her outfit is feminine but practical, loose around the legs but with tight cuffs.

Draw an egg-shaped head with a pointed chin, and a curved spine. Add circles for the shoulders and elbows, and join with lines. Draw two ellipses for the buttocks and a straight line for the waist, and join these to create hips. Draw lines for the legs and triangles for the feet.

Join the head and shoulder line to create a neck. Draw the curve of her visible side, and the breast that can be seen, then flesh out the arms and legs. Note that only one hand can be seen.

With the basic body in place, it's time to add facial details. Give her large eyes, a button nose, and a tiny mouth. Add the ear that can be seen, then give her spiky bangs and use a few pencil lines to indicate hair.

Add clothing details. She has a standup collar and sash trim over her right shoulder. Loose and flowing below-the-knee pants complete her outfit.

MODEL BEHAVIOR

This character is striking a tongue-in-cheek modelling pose, as suggested by one hand on the hip and the other playing with her hair. She's coyly bending her left leg, and she has a happy smiling expression with closed eyes. Note the small, pointed ears, which are a feature on many manga characters, and give a slight fantasy air. Long blazing orange hair completes the look.

Start with an egg shape for the head. Add a center line and a shoulder line. Add circles for the shoulder, hip, knee, and elbow joints, and lines for the limbs.

Flesh out the body, working from the neck along the arms and down the torso and legs. Indicate her breasts. Draw the fingers of her right hand on her hip.

Get some detailing into her face. Her eyes are narrow slits, and her mouth is a grin. Add spiky bangs and knee-length flowing locks down her back.

Add details on the clothes. She is wearing a crop top and shorts with white trimming. Shade these lightly in pencil. Add shoes, and a couple of bangles on her wrist.

Ink, then color your girl. Use pale pink for her skin, leaving white highlights and adding dark beige shadows. Give her striking orange hair, leaving a white highlight on top. To complement the orange, make her suit and pumps acid green.

WALKING ON AIR

Here is a simple but graceful pose, which can be used to indicate a happy carefree mood or a free spirited girl. Her expression is wide-eyed and smiling, and she has one leg bent up at the knee and her arms stretched out wide either side of her, as if she's enjoying the breeze blowing over her. In manga a character can literally defy gravity and walk on air if the mood takes her.

Draw an egg-shaped head and a center line. Bisect this with a horizontal for the shoulders, and two lines for the arms. Draw a triangle for the hips, ovals for the knee joints, and verticals for the legs.

Start to flesh out the figure. Give her a slim neck, ovals for the shoulders, and add the outstretched arms. Her waist is tiny, going into the pelvis. Add legs, and the foot of her right leg.

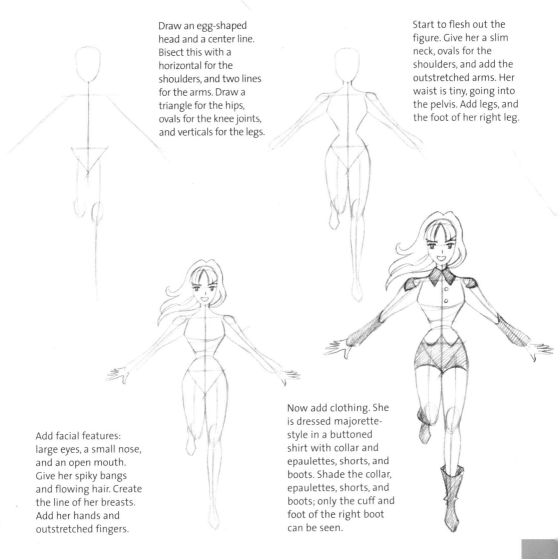

Add facial features: large eyes, a small nose, and an open mouth. Give her spiky bangs and flowing hair. Create the line of her breasts. Add her hands and outstretched fingers.

Now add clothing. She is dressed majorette-style in a buttoned shirt with collar and epaulettes, shorts, and boots. Shade the collar, epaulettes, shorts, and boots; only the cuff and foot of the right boot can be seen.

29

SITTING DAYDREAMING

Nothing beats a quiet moment sitting and daydreaming. Imagine this manga girl sitting on the grass on a cool summer evening. Her hands are clasping her shins and she's looking happily upward at the viewer, with her head tilted backward in an open and relaxed pose.

Draw an oval head, two circles for the two shoulder joints and the hip, a rectangle with a curved profile for the torso, and straight lines for the arms and legs.

Create the basic profile. Her back is a curve: sketch one line joining both shoulder joints, and one from the chin down. Her breast is a curve too. Add the legs.

Make two parallel horizontal lines across her face and use these as guides for her large eyes and tiny ears. Add a nose and mouth, then flesh out the arms.

Start to ink your sketch, concentrating on the most important lines. Add more facial detail, inking the pupils and around the twin highlights in each eye. Outline the mouth and add two or three tiny vertical lines to the nose.

Add spiky bangs, with a ponytail down her back. Then start to indicate her clothing: she is wearing a crop top with detailing around the neck and down the front, and shorts with cuff detail. Indicate the top of her boots.

WIELDING A SWORD

Not all manga girls are shy and fragile creatures, and here is a good example of a confident action girl who is ready for a fight with sword poised. Her stance is balanced with legs apart for stability, and the long sash at her waist is used to give a dramatic effect of movement and tension.

Draw an oval head, and a center line down to a triangle for the pelvis. Add lines for the legs, with ovals for the knee joints. Add oval shoulder and elbow joints.

Add flesh to your basic shape. Join the neck and shoulders, then create a torso, with curved breast and trim waist. Add legs and feet, then the arms.

Work in facial features of eyes, nose, and mouth. Add a spiky hairdo: continue this down to her waist. Draw a sword in her hands, and start to indicate clothing.

The outfit has a bold black and white pattern, so minimal color can be used. Add some light gray shadows to the arms and legs to give depth, then color her face and neck a fleshy pink, with darker beige shadows under the fringe and neck. Use an orange for the pupils, and add some pale mauve shadow to her white hair. Add gold color to the sword hilt, and a rich purple to the sash. Finish with some soft white pencil highlights on the sash and body, and some blue-gray shadows on the blade.

Ink in the main lines of your sketch. Then use a brush pen to color in the black areas of her costume: the fitted top, and the detail on the pants and shoes. There is an area of shadow on the skirt cape, and a fold in its band.

DOWN ON ONE KNEE

A difficult pose to get right is kneeling down, which again requires a good knowledge of your character's body shape. Here is a warrior girl taking a moment of rest. She is propping herself up with her traditional katana sword in its sheath, and surveying the view. Her body is balanced with left knee up and the right on the ground, with her right hand resting across the thigh.

Draw circles for the head, shoulder joints, and one visible elbow, with lines to join the shoulders and for the arms. Draw a curved spine, and an oval for the hip joint. The legs at this stage are both angled lines.

Refine the profile of her face, then add a neck. Add a torso with a trim waist, and two curves for breasts. Flesh out her left arm, adding an outline hand. Next flesh out her legs. Both are bent at the knee: the knee of her right leg is on the ground, while her left knee is in the air, with her foot steadying her. Indicate both feet.

Work next on her facial features. Give her large eyes with double highlights, eyebrows, a snub nose, and small mouth. Add her right ear and flesh out her right arm, adding fingers resting on her left thigh. Now indicate the sword: this runs behind her hand and down to the ground on a plane with her right leg and left toe. Draw a line for the hilt.

Give her a hairband, and then add spiky hair above it and down her back. Now start to get some details into the clothing. Give her a military-style jacket with stand-up collar, fabric closures, and decorative flashes on the sleeves. Her pants also have decorative flashes. Then add detail to the sword.

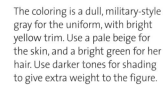

The coloring is a dull, military-style gray for the uniform, with bright yellow trim. Use a pale beige for the skin, and a bright green for her hair. Use darker tones for shading to give extra weight to the figure.

Ink in the main lines of your sketch. Refine the clothing details and add detail to the boots. Create a rectangular pattern on the sword. Next use black to color her pupils, and create the shadow on her neck and on the underside of the hilt.

POPULAR FEMALE POSES

There are several poses that recur in manga time and time again, and it is worth drawing these so that you can tell more of your story through your characters' body language, as well as through their faces and clothes.

below This pose is worried: the girl is anxious and nervous. Her knees are knocked together and she is slightly hunched over in a defensive body position.

above This is a demure, submissive girl in a Japanese kimono. Breaking free of tradition and leading the exciting life of a modern young woman is a common theme.

above Here's a girl who is running away from something in alarm. She is leaning forward and away from the danger, while her eyes are glancing fearfully back toward it.

right Under threat, this girl is poised and ready to defend herself. Her stance is resolute, with her legs set wide apart and her arms crossed in front of her. The hands are ready for action.

left Assertive, but not in the least aggressive, this is a confident pose. The girl is sitting in a comfortable pose, looking happy and slightly mischievous.

below With her feet planted firmly on the floor, and her hand brought up into a fist, this girl has a gutsy air. This is a common pose in manga, designed to say "I did it."

right With fists at the ready and fiery hair, this is a feisty pose. Even though she is wearing a smart dress, this girl is not afraid to get her hands dirty.

left This girl has a wistful pose, as if daydreaming. Her chin is resting on her hands and her knees are together with her feet apart. She's gazing into the distance with a slight smile and her eyes show a hint of concentration.

GALLERY

space walker

above You can tell this girl is cute, even in a space suit. The suit itself is designed to look feminine, but is still functional enough for a space walk.

leaping into action

right This girl is jumping into position with a staff at the ready. Her clothing is cute, but has the look of a military uniform about it. Her expression is determined.

superheroine

above Streaking through the air, this girl is on her way to right some wrongs. She has a typical figure-hugging leotard with a cape, and has long flowing hair to make her more feminine.

boiling hot

right Cowering from a source of great heat, this girl is flushed and there are drops of sweat falling from her hace. All the colors in this sketch suggest heat.

boxer

right Here is a sporty character with spiky, swept-back hair and functional vest and shorts. Her boxing gloves show she's in a fight and the athletic stance says she won't be a pushover.

magical girl

above Girls with amazing powers are popular in the shoujo style of manga. This fairy-like character has insect features.

freezing cold

below This girl is frost-bitten. Her body is thin and she's hugging herself to try and keep warm. Her knees are turned inward and the pale blue lines suggest she is shivering.

schoolgirl

left This typical schoolgirl with sailor-suit type uniform is being surprised by a cute little creature. She has a sweet innocent look that is enhanced by her stance.

RUNNING HEADLONG

With male manga characters, the body can be drawn in a slightly more forceful pose. This example is a young male tearing full-speed into an aggressive position, with fists clenched and head set forward. The leading leg is bent at the knee and is curving outward in a dynamic flowing shape. The torso is nearly horizontal, which emphasizes the onrushing posture.

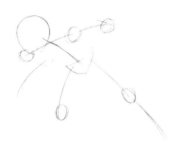

Draw an egg-shaped head with pointed chin. Draw three circles for the two shoulder joints and one visible elbow joint, and join with a curved line. Add a curved line for the spine, and a triangle for the pelvis. Add ovals for knee joints and lines for the legs.

Add flesh to the torso, arms, legs, and feet. Add fists to both arms. Draw in his left ear.

Start to add facial features: large eyes and tiny nose and mouth. Give him some spiky hair. Then start to add costume details. Give him a clenched left fist.

Ink the main lines using a thick nib. Add some creases to his clothes, then use black ink to color his pupils, the shadow under his chin, and his hair.

STRIDING ALONG

This is a more relaxed pose, showing a teenager strolling along in a positive, carefree manner. Remember to have opposite limbs leading, for example: left leg, right arm forward. Both feet are in contact with the ground in this walking pose, with toes on the right leg and heel on the left down, and his arms are swinging loosely by his sides.

Draw an oval head. Add a vertical spine. Bisect this, and add circles for the shoulder and elbow joints with lines for the limbs. Add a triangle for the pelvis, one knee joint, and four lines for the legs.

Add a neck and shoulders, then flesh out the arms. Draw the legs, from the hip joints down to the knee joint: his left leg is in front of his right and moving forward. Add the lower legs.

Give him facial features: eyes with double highlights, and tiny nose and mouth. Add spiky bangs and simple hair. Add hands, one open and one fist.

Outline a circle logo and white cuffs on his teeshirt, then shade the rest. Finally, ink over the main lines, and add detail to his pants and shoes.

STANDING FIRM

Here's a confident, no-nonsense pose for a young male. He's standing tall and straight, with arms folded but a slight tilt to the head, which indicates a cautious manner. The legs are slightly apart too, which gives him a solid, stable stance, as if to imply he's not about to be moved, no matter what happens.

Draw an inverted egg for the head, and a vertical spine, with a triangle for the pelvis. Draw circles for the shoulder, elbow, and knee joints, with lines for the limbs.

Start to flesh out the body. Add a collar, shoulders, torso, and the arms, one folded over the other. Give him flared pants and simply shaped shoes.

Add facial features and outline the spiky hair. Create clothing details: the V-neck, belt, and flashes on the pants and top. Add the soles of the shoes.

Ink all the main lines, then use your black to color the hair, leaving a white flash, and create shadow on the neck and under the arms. Add detail on the knees.

Keep the coloring simple. Use pale pink for the skin of his face, neck, and hands, with a dark beige for shadows. Use a bright blue for his uniform.

RECOIL

This character is pulling back in alarm from some sudden threat or danger. The body is leaning backward, and the leading leg is turned inward in preparation for turning the whole body away. His left arm is pulled back and counter-balancing the sudden shift in weight, and his casual suit is flowing away from the body to exaggerate the movement.

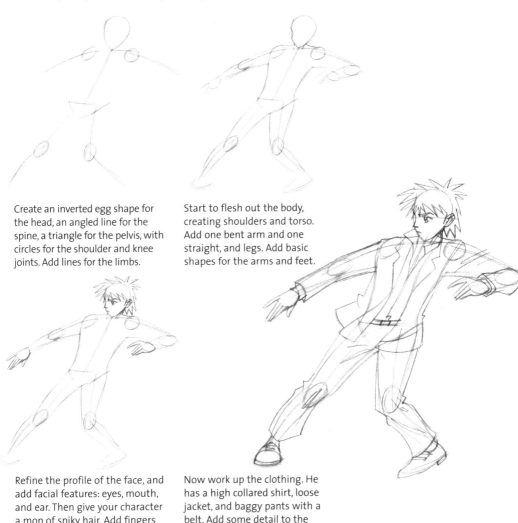

Create an inverted egg shape for the head, an angled line for the spine, a triangle for the pelvis, with circles for the shoulder and knee joints. Add lines for the limbs.

Start to flesh out the body, creating shoulders and torso. Add one bent arm and one straight, and legs. Add basic shapes for the arms and feet.

Refine the profile of the face, and add facial features: eyes, mouth, and ear. Then give your character a mop of spiky hair. Add fingers to both hands.

Now work up the clothing. He has a high collared shirt, loose jacket, and baggy pants with a belt. Add some detail to the shoes on his feet.

ATTACK AND DEFEND

As the saying goes, the best form of defense is attack, and here is an example of a typical action manga character in a battle stance, shield up and sword poised to strike. His rear leg is bent to brace his weight against attack, and to enable him to push forward quickly. He has turned his body side-on to limit the attack area, and his face is set in an angry and defiant snarl.

Use an inverted egg shape for the head, with a circle for his right shoulder joint. Draw a circle for his left elbow joint with two lines for the limb. Draw a center vertical, then obscure most of it with the shape of the shield. His right leg is a single line; his left leg is a Z-shape with a circle for the knee joint.

Now start to flesh out the body. There is a little torso showing on his right-hand side. Add his muscular right arm and clenched right fist in a gauntlet. Draw his left shoulder and the fingers of his left hand, then flesh out his legs, adding heavy boots to both.

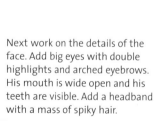

Next work on the details of the face. Add big eyes with double highlights and arched eyebrows. His mouth is wide open and his teeth are visible. Add a headband with a mass of spiky hair.

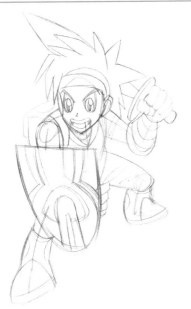

Start to add details. There are several layers of clothing at the neck, in addition to straps for his backpack, and oval motifs on both pant legs. Draw in the sword, and add decorative details to the shield.

Ink the main lines of your drawing and indicate some creases around the knee of his left leg. Then use black to create shadows at the sides of his mouth and on the gauntlet on his left hand.

Give your warrior pale blue eyes and acid green hair, with a brown headband. His skin is pink with a darker pink in his open mouth. Color his costume blue, working over this in shadow areas to strengthen the color. Use a dark leather color for his backpack, then work the boots, shield, and hilt in shades of brown, honey, and yellow. Finally, add ice blue to the blade and gauntlets.

COMING AT YOU

Here is a pose that involves a dynamic body shape with some foreshortening to emphasize the forward movement. The character is running full tilt toward the viewer and letting loose with a flying punch. Note how the forward knee is curved inward, and the trailing leg is smaller to increase the distance from the viewer. The punching arm cuts diagonally across the body.

Draw an inverted egg head with a vertical line down to a triangle for the pelvis. Draw ovals for the elbows, shoulders, and one knee joint, with lines for the limbs.

Flesh out the upper body, adding arms and fists, and the torso. Add eyes and eyebrows, with a small nose and mouth, then draw a crown of spiky hair.

Add his legs; one is drawn from the hip to the knee joint and has only a foot visible. This obscures the full-length right leg. Lightly shade his hair and shorts.

Use a thick nib to ink the main lines. Then color the shorts and hair black. Create a round neck and sleeves for his top. Finally, create a six-pack on his torso.

WIDE POWER STANCE

An altogether different stance is this squatting figure with outstretched arms and wide open hands. The figure is dynamically low to the ground and almost symmetrical in its stability. The outfit suggests a street fighter of some sort, and his stance could be a deflective one, or he could be getting set to unleash some kind of power blast from his open palms.

Bisect an inverted egg head with a curved line and add triangle hands. Add a short line to a triangle pelvis, then add legs and feet in an inverted Z shape.

Create wide shoulders and muscled arms, then a muscular torso down to the waist. Clothe the leg lines with baggy pants that hang in loose folds.

Add facial features: here, slit eyes and an open mouth. Add ears and a simple spiky haircut, then indicate wrist and belly wraps. Add a sash and kung fu slippers.

Ink all the main lines of the sketch. Create detail on the palms, and then indicate lots of folds on the bottoms of the pant legs to get some movement here.

Color his skin pale pink with a darker shade for the open mouth. Give him yellow hair, gray-brown pants and slippers, and a bright red sash.

FLYING PUNCH

The figure in manga can often be graceful and balletic, such as this flying punch pose. It's drawn in profile to get the most out of the action. His clothes are simple and designed for combat, and he's barefoot and bare-armed for an austere, focused appearance.

Draw an oval head with a vertical down to a circle knee joint, and add a line for the lower leg. Add an oval pelvis, a circle and two lines for the leg, and a line and six circles for his shoulder, elbow joints, and fists.

Flesh out the torso, arms, and legs, all of which are muscular. Then, give him an fierce facial profile with feline nose and open mouth. Add an eye and eyebrow, together with an ear.

Add a lion's-mane hairstyle, shaggy on top with a ponytail down his back. Then draw a clenched fist on his left arm, and fingers on his right hand.

Ink the main lines, adding costume details, including torn edges to his shirt and pant legs. Use black to create wristbands, and shadows on his hair and leg.

Color his skin using pink and beige, building shadow as necessary. Make his suit red, with a white highlight on his left thigh. Finally, color his hair in two shades of blue.

THREAT BEHIND

Another type of action pose is this figure, who's turning to face a threat from behind. His long, spidery legs and arms are typical of many manga characters. His weight is balanced evenly between both legs, and his left arm is raised defensively to counter a blow.

Start with an oval head, circles for the shoulder joints, and lines for the shoulders, arms, and spine. Add an ellipse for the hip with lines and circles for the legs.

Flesh out the head and body. The face is in profile: give him a bushy eyebrow, an eye, nose, and mouth. He has a shock of hair and a pumping fist.

Next add clothes to the body. He is wearing a teeshirt, open jacket with high collar and patch details, and tight pants. Draw in his pointed boots.

Begin inking. Go over all the main lines of his face, body, and clothing. Include the creases in his clothes. Ink his eye and eyebrow and his black hair.

Now color your figure. His facé and hands are shades of pink, and his clothes are shades of brown and gray. Color the patches on his sleeves yellow.

JUMPING FOR JOY

Not all manga males are grim fighters. This boy, for example, is a gleeful youth, jumping for joy. He's wearing simple clothing of teeshirt and jeans, and carrying a rucksack, which suggests he's on his way to or from school. The head is drawn larger in relation to the body, which makes him look younger, and his arms and legs have an elastic quality which gives a more cartoony feel.

Draw a round head, a vertical center line, a line for the shoulders with circles for the elbows, a broad ellipse for the pelvis, with circles and lines for the knee joints and legs.

Detail the face which is dominated by the huge open mouth with broad lips. His eyes are simply closed slits with eyebrows. Draw his ears and give him a spiky short hairstyle.

Add flesh to the bones, and give the character some clothes. The shirt is loose and has short sleeves. Draw arms and legs, and simple shapes for hands.

Finish your sketch by giving him pants and shoes, and fleshing out the arms and hands. As a finishing touch, add the straps of a backpack, and shade them.

CREEPING AROUND

Here's another example of a more cute and cartoon-style figure. This character is peering nervously round a corner. His body is bent forward with his weight on the front leg and his left arm cautiously out in front. The figure is supported on the toes of his right boot, and his rear arm is tucked in behind. The eyes are wide open as he peeps round, and his manner suggests someone creeping.

Start with an oval head, with circles for the shoulder, elbow, and hand. Join these with a curved line. Add an ellipse for the hip, circle for the knee, and lines for the leg and foot.

Add details for the face. The eye is large, with a pupil with a highlight. The nose is small and a determined mouth. Give him lots of spiky, cropped hair, outline a highlight, and add an ear.

Now add clothes to the lines of the body. He is wearing a loose hoodie and jeans, which bag below the knees. Add large fingers to his hand, and a sneaker on his foot.

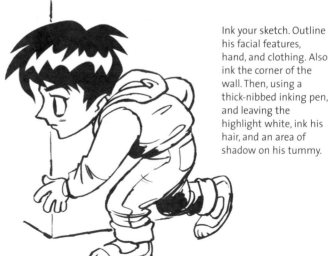

Ink your sketch. Outline his facial features, hand, and clothing. Also ink the corner of the wall. Then, using a thick-nibbed inking pen, and leaving the highlight white, ink his hair, and an area of shadow on his tummy.

His right leg needs to be added now. This is bent back, and also has a jeans leg and sneaker. Finally, at this stage, indicate the corner of a wall: he is looking around this.

PUNCHING AT YOU

This is an unusual pose for a manga story, as it is reminiscent of the mainstream superhero characters in Western comics. It is a useful pose, and worth practicing. The character is flying or leaping toward you with fist outstretched. His outfit is skintight superhero-style.

Draw an oval head and a center line, bisected by a horizontal for the shoulders. Add circles for the shoulder joints, a triangle for the pelvis, and lines for the legs.

Add the basic shape of the arm, then position the fist: this is the focal point of the sketch. Flesh out the body, then clothe the legs and suggest feet.

Next add the facial details: large eyes with double highlights, button nose, and small mouth. Suggest a hairline. Then work up both hands, including the fist.

Use honey and maroon to create his clothing. Leave areas of white highlight on his pants to suggest they are made of a shiny fabric. Leave white areas on his punching fist and around his collar. Color his face pale pink.

Ink the main lines of the figure. Then use black to create shadow under the neck, on the fist, on his right arm, and on his feet. Add his eyes, and hair, with a highlight.

HEROIC POINTING

Another heroic figure, this one is adopting a classic pointing stance. His shape is compact and muscled, as a fighter would be. His right leg is standing braced up on a rock incline, which helps to create a dramatic pose. The outfit is a sleeveless leotard with waistband and headband.

Outline the figure using basic shapes: an oval for the head, shoulder, elbow, and knee joints. Add a triangle for the pelvis, then join all the joint lines.

Start to detail the head, giving your character large eyes, and a small nose and mouth. His hair is a spiky crop, held by a band. Then flesh out the torso and arms.

Next flesh out the legs and feet, which are wide apart. Then add hands. His left hand is pointing, so detail the index finger, and then the other, closed fingers.

Outline his clothing: a tight-fitting cropped vest and tight pants with ankle cuffs. Shade these, then shade his headband. Finally, add shaded wristbands.

NOTHING DOING

A static but powerful pose, this one is useful for situations in which the character needs to stand his ground. The legs are wide apart and ramrod-straight, making a basic A-shape. The arms are folded to present a closed front, and his head is cocked slightly to one side, as if in challenge.

Draw an oval head, add a center vertical, then bisect it with a line for the shoulders. Add shoulder and knee joints, a triangular pelvis, and lines for arms and legs.

Make a line for the eyes and add them, then sketch his face with a pointed chin. Top this with spiky hair. Add flesh to his folded arms, torso, and legs.

Work on the clothing. He has a tight jacket with a high collar, and tight pants that bag around the knee where they fit into boots. Add a crossed belt.

Ink your sketch, adding fold lines on the sleeves and pants. Accent the foot of the boots. Then add shadows around the collar, under the folded arms, and on the boots.

Color his teeshirt black, then color your figure's head pink. Give him red hair. Use gray for his suit. Finally add yellow details on his suit, and color his boots yellow with brown shadows.

FALLING CAT JUMP

This is a dramatic posture, showing a young, athletic fighter falling from above. His arms are raised like a cat, and the shoulders sit high in line with the head to give power to the pose. The legs are split: the right is stretched out ready to land and the left is folded for aerodynamic shape.

Start with an egg shape on its side for the head. Draw one circle above this and one below for the elbow joints, with lines for the arms and a circle for his fist. Add a large oval for his hip. Draw circles for his knee joints and lines for legs and feet.

Create arms and flesh out the torso. Draw his left leg from the hip to the knee joint, then out to the shoe line. Add a shoe. Draw his right leg behind the left. Add his facial features, then give him some spiky hair. Shade this.

He is wearing a loose top with tight cuffs and swinging toggles, loose pants that bunch down his right leg, and martial arts slippers. Draw a sash around his waist, folds and creases in his clothing, and then draw clenched fists.

Ink the main lines, including the creases in his top. Then use black to color his pupils, his hair, and his pants. Leave white highlights down the front of both legs. Color the shadow under his chin and his slippers black too.

Now use a combination of pink for his skin and dark beige for shadows on his face, hands, and feet. Use a fresh apple-green to color his top and toggles, then use a blue-gray to tone down the highlights on his pants. Finally add a little pale gray to his sash to indicate shadows.

GALLERY

speeding at you

right With a figure that is running like this one, you can enhance the sense of movement by adding speed lines.

subtle

above Coloring can be subtle and still effective. Use cool, dark colors for jackets and trousers, then add some bright touches, such as red for a teeshirt.

unruffled

right This character is calm, confident, and fully aware of the turmoil he is causing to all the young girls around him.

well held

above Add to the dynamism of a leap into the air by adding whoosh lines around the arm.

full of joy

left This character is overjoyed, as evidenced by the huge grin from ear to ear and the jumping figure. The whoosh lines magnify the action.

raging

below Body language can show how a character is feeling. This one is in a rage, with clenched fists and flushed cheeks.

with a pet

left Cute pets are common in manga, and this character is delighted to be playing with his friendly puppy.

Faces

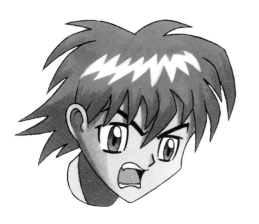

The face is the key to any visual medium, and particularly with a static graphic medium like manga. The reader must be able to tell at a glance the personality, emotion, and intentions of any character, and a good artist can portray this. This chapter shows the basic construction of faces, together with a range of expressions you will find useful.

FRONT VIEW

Here's a basic front view of a female face. Most faces are pretty much symmetrical, and the ears, eyes, and nose follow a fairly consistent pattern, with the tops of the ears in line with the top of the eyes, and the nose halfway down again toward the chin. The position of the mouth can vary from character to character, but here it sits just over halfway between the nose and chin.

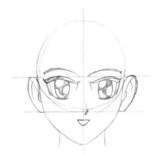

Draw a simple circle, then draw down diagonal lines for the cheeks before turning in and coming to a curving point for the chin. Add a vertical center line, with lines for the neck below.

The eyes are the key in manga faces, so start with these: black pupils with dual highlights. Position the nose, ears, and mouth. Add in eyebrows.

Now add the hair, starting with the chunky bangs. Then, from a center line, take the hair up and bring it down to below chin level. Don't make this too detailed.

Add color, using pale pink for her face, with beige for shadow areas in the ears, under the bangs, in the mouth, and under the chin. Use beige too for the right pupil, and to outline the eyes. Finally, outline a white highlight in the bangs, and color the rest of the hair a vibrant purple.

Ink the main lines, using a thin pen for the eyes, nose, and mouth, with a thicker nib for the outline of the face and the hair. Keep the bangs and hair separate. Color the pupils black.

PROFILE

Now take the same character and draw it from the side. The relative positions of the eyes, nose, and mouth should be the same. Note how the face outline goes in for the eye area before curving out to a point for the nose, then sloping back diagonally down to the chin. Manga noses are usually tiny and pointed, like this one.

 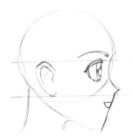 

Start with a circle, then draw a V to make the chin. Add a line for the back of the neck. Then create an indentation and a point to get the profile of the nose.

Add horizontal lines to help with positioning: the ear and eye sit on this line. The double highlight is visible from this angle. Refine the nose and add the mouth.

Draw the hair in two pieces. The bangs form a semicircle, with narrow V-shapes cut in. Draw the curve of the rest of the hair, down to below chin level.

Color the face pale pink and add beige shadows under the bangs inside the ear, above and below the eye, inside the mouth, and under the chin. Finally, outline a white highlight in the hair, and color the rest of the hair vivid purple.

Now ink your sketch. Ink around the face, and the two separate blocks of hair. Use a fine pen to outline the mouth. Then color the pupil black.

LOOKING UPWARD

This face is looking upward at an angle to the top left. You can see the ears are lower with respect to the eyes, and the pupils are raised to the top part of the eye to give a line of vision in that direction. The sharply drawn eyebrows indicate concern and anxiety, while the open mouth suggests she is calling or shouting out.

Draw an oval head, and bisect it horizontally with a curved line nearer the top. Bisect it vertically with a curve nearer to one side than the other. Add the neck.

Sit the pupils on the horizontal line. Add large eyes with double highlights. The visible ear comes from this line too. Sit the nose and mouth on your vertical line.

Next add the hair. This is short and spiky. Create three pieces for the bangs and front of the hair, and then draw the rest of the hair, starting from the crown.

Outline an area of highlight on each of the bangs. Finally, loosely shade the hair, using a very soft pencil, and shade inside the mouth.

BATTLE CRY

This is a powerful face with mouth open in an aggressive cry, shown by the downturn at the corners of the mouth, and the heavy black eyebrows pointing down to the center. Strong black lines around the eyes increase the intensity of the expression. Her left shoulder is raised and pulled across her face slightly, which suggests she is preparing to deliver a blow.

Start with a pointed oval. Bisect it horizontally and vertically. Create a curve for the front shoulder, a vertical for the neck, and a curve for the other shoulder.

Draw the large eyes with three areas of highlight, and add arched eyebrows. Add the ears, and a small nose. Then draw the large open mouth.

Add the spiky profile of the hair inside the oval. Then give her a long ponytail with a flicked end. Outline a couple of highlights. Then indicate the clothing.

Ink all the main lines, including the folds in the clothes. Then use black to color the hair and the pupils. Finally create the shadow inside the mouth and under the chin.

SMOLDERING FRUSTRATION

Here's another angry expression—this time the face is pointing downward and the eyes are looking angrily up, to give a feeling of barely controlled frustration. The eyes are narrowed and her cheeks are flushed, with the mouth a tiny oval. The sloping hair accentuates the forward tilt of the head.

Start with an egg shape and bisect it horizontally and vertically to help with positioning the features. Add the neck, and bisect this too.

Add the features, starting with the eyes with double highlights. Add arched eyebrows, then the one visible ear. Add a pert nose and a tiny open mouth.

Give the head some hair next. Work spiky bangs from the top of the oval, and continue it outside the edge of the face. Then add the long locks.

Ink all the main lines, including the areas of detail on the hair. Use a fine pen for the nose and mouth. Then color the pupils black.

Color her face pale pink, using a darker pink for the flush in her cheeks, in her mouth, and under her chin. Give her blue pupils and a mass of yellow hair.

ICY GLARE

The face here is that of a typical cold-hearted female, with an icy stare. The dark, narrow eyes and the thin closed lips mean nothing but trouble. The chin is a sharper point than that of most females, which gives a meaner feel to her face, and the cascading black spikes of her hair are almost spider-like.

Draw a circle, then bisect it vertically. Continue this line down, then sketch two lines to form a V-shape at its base: this will be the chin of the character.

Start to add features, beginning with the eyes and arched eyebrows. Give the figure a small nose and a cupid's bow mouth with a sardonic smile.

Add in the two lines of a hairband across the head, then add the bangs out from this. Then, working from the crown, add the mass of spiky hair.

Ink the main lines of the face, and the upstanding collar. Use a fine pen for the nose and mouth. Then use black to color the hair around the areas of highlight.

Now add color. Here the face is pink, with darker shadows on the sides and under her chin. Make her hairband bright green, and her top purple. Finally give her red lips.

63

BABY FACE

Faces can be a good way to show the age of a character. This face is small and wide, so it makes for a younger look. The features are close together in the middle of the face, like a baby's, and she has a petulant expression, with an open, sulky mouth and arched eyebrows.

Draw an oval, with a pointed end. Bisect this with a curved horizontal and a curved vertical: these will help you to position the facial features. Then add a short vertical to indicate a neck.

Start with the eyes, using your curved horizontal as their base. Outline the pupils and give them highlights. Then add arched brows. Use your curved vertical to position the nose and mouth.

Now add hair. Make this a short, spiky style, with chunky bangs and off-center part. Outline a highlight and a clip on the hair. Then add eyelashes.

Ink over the main lines, using a thick nib for the outline, hair, ear, and eye and eyebrow. Use a thinner nib for the nose and mouth. Color the pupils black.

Use shades of beige for the face, with darker shades for the shadow areas under the bangs and chin. Color the pupils honey, then give the figure red hair with a yellow clip.

SAD CONTEMPLATION

This face has a mood of calm but with a sense of unhappiness, indicated by the tightly closed lips and the lightly drawn eyebrows. Her eyes are closed, as shown by the under-arching black lines and the eyelashes, and her hair falls lifelessly down and is a somber white color.

Start by drawing an oval, and bisect this with a straight vertical. Draw down to this line to make a chin. Then bisect your circle with a horizontal.

Use your horizontal to position the closed eyes and the ears. Add eyebrows, then use your vertical line to position the slightly snubbed nose and thin mouth.

Add the hair next. Use the top of your oval as the line to start your bangs, which are a few thick chunks. Then create the profile of the rest of the hair.

Now ink all the main lines. The eyelashes are one of the dominant features, and the rest of the face and hair are deliberately kept quite simple.

Finally add some color. Use pale pink for the skin, with dark beige for shadow areas in the ears, under the bangs, around the nose and mouth, and under the chin. Then use a cool gray to add shadow to the hair.

DREAMY LONGING

Another closed-eye expression, this one has a wistful, dreamy quality. The head is tilted back and slightly to one side, and the eyebrows are sloping upward. The corners of the mouth are turned up in a hint of a smile. Note the low position of the ear which emphasizes the angle of the tilt of the head.

Start with an off-center oval as your basic shape. Bisect this horizontally and vertically with curved lines.

Position the main features along your bisecting lines. These include the eyes and the visible ear, together with the nose and mouth. Add eyebrows.

Create spiky bangs with four or five bold points, then add the profile of the rest of the hair, giving it short spiky ends.

Ink over the main lines of the face and hair. At this stage, add highlights in the hair to leave white later.

Color the skin pale pink, with dark pink for the shadow in the mouth, under the bangs, and under the chin. Then, leaving the highlights white, give her blue hair.

UNWELCOME SURPRISE

This face has a look of startled alarm on it. The eyes are wide open, and slightly downturned. The mouth is also down at the sides, which tells the viewer that the surprise is undoubtedly an unwelcome one. The hairstyle in this case frames the startled eyes nicely, and draws the viewer's attention into the face.

Start with an oval, then work a couple of lines down to a smooth pointed chin. Bisect this oval with curved horizontal and vertical lines.

Add the main features, starting with the eyes. These are wide open, with lots of white around the pupils. Add a tiny snub nose and an open mouth.

Next give the head some hair. Start this higher than the basic oval, and keep the lines smooth and flowing.

Ink the sketch. Outline the face and its features, as well as the hair. Use black to outline the eyes and to color the pupils, which have a highlight.

Finally, color the sketch. Give your figure pale pink skin, with beige shadows under the bangs, along the right-hand jawline, and under the chin. Then give her auburn hair and pale green eyes.

HOPEFUL STARE

Some expressions can be extremely subtle, and these are needed in manga comics where the stories can be complex. The face here is staring head-on at the viewer and shows a hint of hope. The eyes and eyebrows are fairly noncommittal, but the mouth is key. A slight upturn at the corners is hopeful, whereas a slight downturn would change the expression to slight despair.

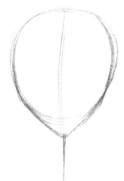

Draw an oval, then work a vertical line to bisect it. Draw two curving lines down to a pointed chin on the vertical. Finally for this stage, draw a curved horizontal line.

Add the facial features. Position the eyes, with double highlights, and ears on the horizontal line. Work a small nose and mouth on the vertical line.

Then add the hair: keep this fairly simple. Outline a jagged highlight across the top.

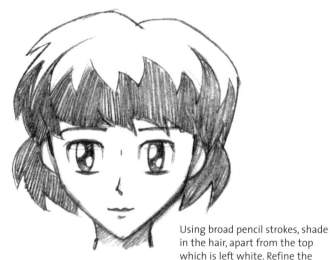

Using broad pencil strokes, shade in the hair, apart from the top which is left white. Refine the color in the pupils, then add shading to the neck.

HAPPY EXPECTATION

Here is a more positive expression of happiness. The head is turned to a three-quarter angle and is gazing up into the sky. Her eyes are large and healthy-looking, and she has a cute rounded girlish face and features. Her red hair and girlish pigtails emphasize the happy-go-lucky and easy-going expression.

Start by drawing a circle, then bring lines down either side to form a soft chin at the bottom right. Indicate a vertical line for the neck.

Draw another horizontal parallel to, but higher than, the first. Also draw in a curved vertical line to bisect the face.

Add eyes with double highlights across your horizontal line, and draw eyebrows. Use your vertical line as a guide for positioning the nose.

Position an ear across the horizontal line. Then add spiky bangs by drawing in some broad Vs. Add some tufts of hair to the left and right of the head.

Next add pigtails, held in place with bobble details. Outline an area of highlight on top of the head.

Use a fine pen to ink over the main lines of the face and hair. Working around the highlights, color the pupils black.

Color your sketch. Use pale pink for the skin, with a darker shade in the ears and on and around the chin. Give the head bright red hair, with green bobbles that secure her pigtails.

GALLERY

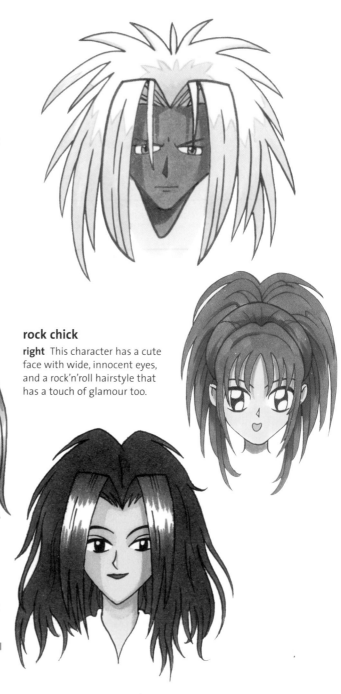

far out

right Dramatic characters need dramatic coloring. Here the dark skin and brooding eyes are complemented by the shock of white hair.

rebellious

below Wide eyes and mouth, together with a cropped, spiky hairstyle position this young, lively character as something of a rebel.

rock chick

right This character has a cute face with wide, innocent eyes, and a rock'n'roll hairstyle that has a touch of glamour too.

strong

right Flowing locks colored dark green and gray add an air of strength to this character. She could be a fighter in a traditional manga action story.

punk

above Spiky hair contributes to a punk look, and this boy's wide-open eyes and sneering mouth add to the defiant impression.

free spirit

above Bright blue is a good hair color for a punky hairstyle. This wide-eyed character is feisty and free-spirited.

pensive

above The head on one side shows a thoughtful nature, a look emphasized by his eyes, staring in the same direction as his head is cocked.

tender

left This character's look is fairly neutral: he may be paying attention or may not. His face shows a sympathetic expression.

youthful

above Large, innocent blue eyes, and plaits of pigtails tend to say a character is young and vulnerable. The blonde hair adds to this effect.

MALE FRONT VIEW

When drawing a male face, the same basic rules apply as to the female, with some significant differences. The jawline is more chiselled, with sharper lines and a squared-off base. The eyes also may be slightly smaller than those of a female, the mouth slightly larger, and the neck wider.

Start with an oval for the head, and bring this to a squared-off chin. Draw a central vertical line to help with positioning.

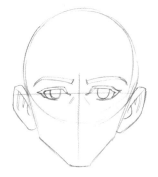

Draw a horizontal across the face and position the eyes across it. Add eyebrows above the eyes, and then position the ears using the same horizontal.

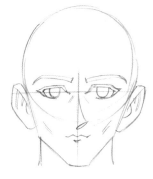

Use your vertical line as a guide for positioning the nose and mouth. Then sketch in a couple of lines to suggest the contours of the cheekbones.

Add hair. Draw spiky bangs across the front of the head. Then create the rest of the hair from a point on the crown out to the left and right.

Ink the main lines, working the hair as a single entity. Establish the eyebrows with two lines, and color the pupils black around the highlights.

Now add color. Use a pale pink for the face, with a darker shadows in the ears. Give him pale blue eyes, and color the hair in two shades of brown.

MALE PROFILE

Here is the same face, but in profile. The features should all be in the same relative positions as in the front view. Note how the brow juts out above the eye, and the nose goes to a sharp point. The top lip should overhang the bottom slightly, and the jaw should step up in angles to the ear.

Start with a circle, then draw a rough triangle down to make a pointed chin. Add a vertical for the back of the neck.

Refine the profile, giving your figure a pointed nose, small mouth, and pointed chin.

Create a horizontal around which to position the visible eye and ear. Add a double line for the eyebrow, and a couple of lines to suggest the cheekbone.

Create the hair, working from a point on the crown forward and back to make a short, spiky, cropped style.

Ink the main lines of your sketch. Double-outline the eye, and draw the black pupil. Erase any pencil lines as you no longer need them.

His skin is pale pink, with darker beige areas of shadow in his ears, under the bangs, and under the chin. Color his hair using two shades of brown.

LOOKING-DOWN TILT

This head is tilted gently away from the viewer, and looking down with a wry smile. Notice the relative positions of the eyes, and how the hair is falling down in a line to follow the tilt. This character's mouth is closed, with a slight upturned smile, and a small shadow under the bottom lip to create a slight pout.

Draw a circle, then add a triangle to make a pointed chin. Add a curving line for the neck.

Add a curved horizontal, then position the eyes on this line. Add eyebrows, then use the bottom of your first circle as the line for the nose.

On the same line as the eyes, add the ear. Then add the mouth underneath the nose.

Draw spikes of hair, working from the crown and across and down to make bangs.

Using a soft pencil and broad strokes, start to shade the eyes and eyebrows. Flesh out the mouth, then shade the spikes of hair, leaving the crown white.

JOYFUL SHOUT

Here's a more animated face, with bright smiling eyes and an open mouth. A hint of the upper teeth helps to give an impression of laughter. This face has soft, youthful curves, which give the character a younger personality.

Start with a circle, then draw a triangle to create a pointed chin.

Bisect your oval both horizontally and vertically to give yourself guides for positioning the features.

Use the horizontal line to position the eyes, with dual highlights, and also the one visible ear. Add a button nose and open mouth.

Give your character spiky cropped hair, working a jagged line across the forehead, and then spikes from the crown.

Ink the main lines, outlining an area of highlight in the hair. Then color the pupils and eyebrows black.

Color the face pale pink, with a darker pink inside the mouth. Then make the area of hair outside the highlight black.

Finally, add shadow inside the ear and under the chin, then color the white highlight in the hair brown.

DISMAY

This face is really down in the dumps. The eyebrows, eyes, and mouth are all pointing down, and the eyes are wide open and staring. The mouth has dropped to a low position on the face, and there are double lines underneath the eyes to suggest wrinkles. The hair emphasizes the look by falling straight down in strands.

Start with a circle, then draw a triangle down to make a pointed chin. Add a vertical here.

Draw the eyes, adding a double highlight in each. Then add eyebrows. Add ears to the same line as the eyes.

Add a tiny nose, then add an open mouth. Refine the ears.

Create a spiky hairstyle by working bangs, then start from the crown and work to left and right. Outline a highlight across the top of the hair.

Ink all the important lines, then use black to color the pupils, except the highlights, and the hair, again leaving the highlight white.

PROFILE WITH FOCUS

Here's an example of how positioning and angle can give meaning to a face. Although this is a normal profile view, the forward angle of the neck and narrowed eyes lend an air of intent to this red-headed male character. The nose exaggerates this by being a sharper point than usual, and the loose hair dropping vertically frames it nicely.

Start with a circle, then draw two lines to come to a point for the chin.

Create the profile by making an indentation for the eye, and adding a snub nose, and slightly open mouth.

Add the eye and eyebrow, based on your horizontal line. Use this line as the midline for the ear.

Now add hair. Start from the crown and work in both directions. Outline an area of highlight on the top.

Ink the outline of the face and hair. Ink the eye and the eyebrow, as well as the ear.

Introduce some color, using a flat pink for the face and bright orange for the hair.

Finally, add more detail to the color. Create shade under the chin, and under the bangs. There is also an area of shadow in the ear.

EXASPERATION

You can make your character more masculine by having a wider, squared-off jaw and a broad neck. This face could belong to a muscle-bound hero or a villain. His head is topped by a hard-looking hairstyle, and his eyes are ringed by heavy black linework and severe eyebrows. The pupils are small black circles, which give a cold touch to the face.

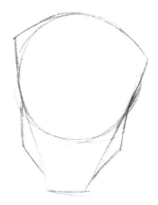

Start by drawing a circle for the head, then draw two lines down, and one horizontal to square off the chin.

Define the shape of the head a little more, squaring off the top and the jawline.

Draw a vertical center line and a curved horizontal to help position the features. Add the large eyes with small pupils, knitted eyebrows, and the nose.

Add the ears, positioning them on the line of your horizontal. Then add the mouth.

Around the existing profile, add in the hairline. Then using broad strokes with a soft pencil, shade this in. As a finishing touch, refine the shape of the mouth.

CONFIDENT SMILE

This character has an intelligent, knowing smile on his face. The head is tilted slightly down so he has to look through his fringe, which makes him look slightly sinister. The eyes are almond-shaped with dark lashes, and he has long, slender, arched eyebrows. His mouth has the smallest of dimples on one side, which can be used to denote a smirk.

Start by drawing a circle, then add two lines to create the profile of the chin.

Add curved horizontal and vertical lines to help with positioning the facial features.

Outline the eyes, then add in eyebrows.

Get some detail into the eyes by working the pupils, leaving a double highlight in each one. Then add the nose.

Next add some hair. Make this a short, spiky style, and indicate a highlight across the top of the head.

Ink all the main lines, making sure that the bangs sit on top of the eyebrows. Color the pupils black, except for the double highlights.

Make his face pale pink, with browner shadows beneath the bangs, in the ear, and below the chin. Then, working around the highlight, color the hair black.

ALARM CALL

Looking up and across in alarm, this face is dramatic and engaging. The upturned angle gives the character a vulnerable look, and the small lines on each cheek suggest a flush of anxiety. Small pupils in the center of the whites of the eyes accentuate the look of fear on his face.

Draw an oval to start the basic head, then add two lines to make a point for the chin.

Create a horizontal and a vertical center line, then outline eyes on the horizontal. Add eyebrows and a nose.

Add an ear, using the horizontal line as a guide to positioning. Then add an open mouth.

Now add a mass of spiky hair. Work from the ear across the forehead to create bangs, then add spikes on top of the head. Draw in the pupils.

Ink your sketch. Break the lines of the eyebrows so that the bangs sit on top of them. Add shading details to the cheeks, and inside the mouth.

GOOFY GRIN

This is a difficult but very effective expression. A grin can indicate embarrassment when coupled with sluggish eyes and flushed cheeks. Note how the teeth are shown clenched in a forced and unnatural manner, and the eyebrows are rising in a hopeful way.

Draw a circle to start with, then add two lines to make a point for the chin.

Bisect the head with a vertical and a horizontal line to help you to position the features.

Start with the eyes, adding pupils with double highlights. Then add eyebrows.

Now draw the nose and mouth. The mouth here is large and open, and, unusually, has clearly defined teeth.

From a center line draw two uprights, then create two areas of spiky bangs. Add hair to the top and back of the head.

Ink all the important lines of the sketch and color the pupils black. Then use black to create the darkest area of hair.

Use pale pink for the face, then add shadow with a dark beige under the bangs, in the ear, and under the chin. Leaving white highlights, color the hair blue.

GRIEF AND MISERY

Some days are better than others, and this shows one of the bad ones. This face is creased and crumpled with crying. The tears streaming from his tightly closed eyes, and the grimace on his mouth show this character is suffering. Tears can be drawn rolling down the cheeks to the chin, for maximum effect.

Draw a circle, then add two lines coming to a point to create the shape of the chin.

To help with positioning the features, bisect your head with a vertical and a horizontal.

Start with the eyes, even though these are squeezed shut. Draw them as curled lines, then add the eyebrows.

Next add the nose and mouth. The mouth is open and the teeth are visible, although undefined.

Then add the visible ear, and use this to help you to add spiky cropped hair.

Create the tears coming from his eyes. Finally, leaving areas of white highlight, lightly shade your character's hair.

REALIZATION DAWNS

This character has just realized his mistake, and feels a definite sense of chagrin about it. His deadpan expression and dilated pupils make him look stunned, and the position of his mouth, represented by a narrow downward-curving line, enforces his dismay.

Begin by drawing a circle, then add a U-shape to create the line of the chin.

Create a horizontal for the eyeline, then add large, open eyes with a small circular pupil.

Use the same horizontal to guide you in placing the ears. Then add a small nose and small, thin, down-turned mouth.

Add a headband, then work spiky bangs from this right across the forehead.

Add more spiky hair on top of the head, taking this over the line of the headband too.

Ink all the lines, making sure you establish where the hair sits on top of the band.

Introduce some color. Use pale pink for the face, with beige shadows. Make the band blue, and color the hair in tones of brown and green.

AN EAR IN DETAIL

As well as the overall face, it's worth taking a moment to look at how the individual features are constructed. The hardest of these is possibly the ear, as we spend the least time looking at it! Everyone's ears are different, but there are general features that you can use to make your character's ear look credible.

Start with two circles, one bigger than the other. Join them with a vertical line.

Refine the main outline of the ear, all around.

Echo this shape inside to create the fold of the ear. Then draw a semicircle and add some other detailing inside the ear.

Take the same ear and draw it from a three-quarter angle by compressing the whole shape sideways.

The profile of the ear from behind is simpler. Draw a narrow C-shape, with a line down it to create the fold at the edge of the ear. Add light shading.

AN EYE IN DETAIL

The eye is a more familiar shape, the most important one in a manga face. Eyes are usually extremely large and glossy-looking, with highlights and graceful lashes. This is a typical example which could be used on all kinds of characters.

Start with a rough saucepan shape, adding small spikes in the top two corners.

Within the saucepan, draw two curving verticals for the pupils, and an oval shape inside that.

Next, define three areas for highlights, overlapping the pupil.

Shade the drawing using darker tones for the pupil and edges of the eye.

Finally, add some sweeping eyelashes and an arched eyebrow.

EXPRESSIONS

A good way to practice expressions is to use the same head, and vary the eyes and mouth to create different looks, as has been done here and opposite. You can also see from these expressions how shading can be used in different positions to vary the facial expression. Draw a series of outline heads and hair, and practice.

This is a dejected expression: the dropped eyebrows and down-sloping eyes, sidelong glance, and worry lines all point to dejection.

A determined expression is characterized by drawn-down eyebrows and flat, hooded tops to the eyes.

An open, laughing mouth and closed eyes with raised eyebrows show that this character is in a happy mood.

This character has a horrified expression. The eyes are huge, but the pupils are tiny dots. The mouth is twisted in a terrified yell.

With eyebrows and eyes sloping upward, this character is smitten. The pupils have bee replaced by hearts to add to the effect.

The perfect oval of the mouth, the wide-open eyes, and the raised eyebrows show that this character has been surprised.

EMOTIONS

You will only get emotion into your characters by practicing. Look at the examples here and pinpoint the major features that characterize each emotion. The eyes are always important and the mouth can be a critical feature. The same basic face here is used to convey six totally different emotions from overjoyed to furious.

This girl is furious. The shape of the eyes, and the arched eyebrows, and the tight, down-curving mouth are ample demonstration of her fury.

Surprise can be indicated by the round, staring eyes and small pupils. The shading lines under the eyes denote a slight anxiety or nervousness.

The large, smiling mouth and closed eyes with downward curves suggest this girl is extremely happy. The shading on the nose makes it look cute.

This girl is alluring: her dark, smoldering eyes with large pupils, and her feminine lips point to her being a seductress.

Chagrin is a difficult emotion to convey. Here the closed eyes on an upward curve denote shameful embarrassment.

Happy, calm, and placid is a useful emotion for many characters. This wide-eyed girl has an innocent expression.

Hair

Hair is another distinctive trait of manga art, and getting a good hairstyle can play a big role in getting your character right. It's rooted in reality: the hair has to flow and fall as it does in life. But your imagination plays a huge part: opt for vibrant colors and big styles, or keep it short and dark. There is plenty to get you started in this chapter.

ORANGE BOB

This is a straightforward shoulder-length cut with full bangs. It's softly feminine but can be used on a harder-edged character if needed, so it's very flexible and a good one to practice. The orange color makes it very striking, and a glossy white highlight makes it look like a healthy head of hair.

Draw a basic head with large eyes, nose, mouth, and one ear. Then create spiky bangs across the front of the head.

Add the rest of the hair, working from the line of the bangs downward. You want to make the hair fall in thick strands, so you need to make very few lines.

Now outline an area of highlight on the top of the head. Keep the lines bold to work with the rest of the hairstyle.

Ink over the main lines of the hair, including the accent lines you created.

Outline the area of highlight above the bangs, then color the rest of the hair bright orange. Go over the color again toward the tips of the hair and bangs to make it darker.

GREEN AND SPIKY

This is a more feisty-looking cut. The large front part is divided into symmetrical bangs is a very popular style in manga. The back is cut quite bushy and short for a tomboyish look, and the color is a very bold shade of green, which is also very popular with manga characters. The key is getting the bangs to look right.

Work a basic head, with eyes, nose, mouth, and one ear. Then, create the front of the hairstyle: this sweeps back from a center part, and folds down in front of the ears on both sides.

Now bisect the top of the head with lines running from front to back and from side to side. Add a spiky outline profile to the top of the head and down the figure's left-hand side.

Next add some spiky hair to the front of the head, to sit behind the upswept strands. Outline areas of highlight on the strands that hang down.

Start to ink the hairstyle. Ink the individual lines of the upsweep, then outline the spikes hanging down in front of the ears, and the rest of the hairstyle.

Create a dramatic color scheme. Use brown for the upsweep and the very tips of hair. Use an acid green for the crown of the head and the front strands, working around the white highlights. Finally, add a darker green to the area you outlined behind the upsweep, on the top of the head.

CENTER PART

This style has a slightly more severe look, but it is still a pretty and tidy hairstyle. The hair is parted in a sharp divide and swept back behind the ears, leaving a nicely exposed face. It's not too fussy, so it could be used on an action-type character or on a businesswoman. The hair is bright blue, but not too outlandish.

Draw a basic head with eyes, nose, mouth, and ear. Add a center line on top of the head.

From this line, create a cupid's bow, from which the hair falls down to the ear level.

Add a couple of lines to define the area above the ear. Then add large individual spikes to the ends of the hair on both sides.

Outline an area of highlight on top of the head on each side of the center part.

Start to ink, outlining the profile of the hair, the center part, a couple of strands above the ear, and a spike in front of the ear.

Color the hair in shades of blue. Leave the highlights you outlined white, then add pale blue around them. Next make areas of darker blue on the ends of the hair.

WITH HAIRBAND

There are lots of ways you can dress up the hairstyles on your characters to give them individuality and style. Here we have a wide elasticated hairband which sits across the bangs and under the body of the hair at the back. The cut itself is fairly neat and frames the face nicely on either side, with a rich green color.

Work a basic head, with eyes, nose, mouth, and ear. Start the hairstyle with a wide hairband across the top of the head.

Next add a spiky fringe below the hairband. Keep the spikes chunky: you only need three or four above each eye.

Now create the outline of the hair itself. There are a couple of spikes on the crown, then the hair falls loosely to about shoulder level.

Outline two areas of spiky highlight on both sides of the hair, one near the top and one closer to the tips.

Start to ink. Work around the profile of the hair, the spiky bangs, and the hairband. Ink behind the hairband, where the fringe falls from.

Color the highlights using a pale green, then choose a darker green for the rest of the hair. Finally color the hairband brown.

BLACK AND SPIKY

For a more dynamic image, you can give your character a spiky, boyish cut like this one. The overall shape is a wedge, with heavy spiked bangs swept forward and over the ears. This type of hairstyle is popular with both sexes in manga, and this one is colored a traditional black.

Draw a basic head, with eyes, nose, mouth, and ear. Then create spiky bangs across the face to the ear.

Add a slightly off-center part, and, from the crown, work down into short spikes on both sides. Add a couple of spikes below ear level on both sides.

Outline a dramatic jagged area of highlight close to the part on both sides.

Ink the part, and then ink around the spiky profile of the hair and bangs.

Color this style dramatic black. Work around the highlights you outlined, and leave a small strip next to the part white too.

BLONDE SWEPTBACK BOB

This is a much more feminine and pretty cut. The hair is swept back from the forehead to an invisible hairband, from where the body of the hair falls down to shoulder-level in a gentle sweep. The corn-yellow color suggests a sweet and innocent personality.

Create a basic head with eyes, nose, mouth, and ear. Then add a sweptback hairline across the front of the head.

Add the crown, with a suggestion of a part, and add hair down to below chin level, creating spiky ends.

Next outline a highlight across the head, behind the bangs, and continue it to the edge of the hair on the right.

Start to ink. Ink around the bangs and across the top of the head, then outline the profile of the hair and the part.

Leave the highlight white, then color most of the hair yellow. Finally, color the tips of the bangs and the hair bright orange.

CURLY PONYTAIL

Here is another feminine hairstyle perhaps for a more mature female character. It has full bushy bangs falling down to the eye-level, and a high, full ponytail falling down at the back, before curling up at the end. This is a style that can be endlessly varied in terms of color, to suit lots of different characters.

Create a basic head with eyes, nose, mouth, and ear. Add a closely spiked bangs, with more, widely spaced spikes falling from the top of the head.

Now add some wider-spaced locks from the top of the head, and falling down to shoulder level. Finish with an upflick.

Outline an area of highlight behind the bangs. Make the spikes of this area echo the spikes of the bangs.

Start to ink. Ink those lines you drew first, then work the locks from the top of the head, and finally those down the back to the upflick.

Next outline the highlight behind the bangs.

Color the area of highlight in a mid red-brown, color the rest of the hair with a slightly darker shade, then use a dark brown for the tips of the bangs and hair.

PINK PIGTAILS

Many female manga girls are young and fun-loving. A typical hairstyle for this type of girl could be these huge pink pigtails, held up on either side of the head by ties. The size is exaggerated for visual effect, and the bright pink color makes for a high-visibility image. The hair is drawn to look slightly shaggy, with lots of movement.

Draw a basic head with eyes, nose, mouth, and ear. Add chunky, spiky bangs across the face: you only need about half a dozen spikes.

Add a couple of pigtails, one on either side of the head, falling down in loose spiky locks. Secure each with a scrunchie.

Create a highlight behind the bangs, from scrunchie to scrunchie. Then outline a highlight on each pigtail.

Start to ink, inking the points of the bangs, the top of the head, the scrunchies, and the pigtails. Add a couple of loose strands on each pigtail.

Next, ink the highlights. Choose a violet pen for this: this will help when you come to color.

Color the hair bright pink, up to the highlights. Finally, add some violet tips to the bangs.

WILD SPIKES

This is a dramatic look with a windswept crown of thick spikes. It would indicate a boyish, sparky female with a big personality. The white highlight on top of the head emphasizes the upsweep of the spikes behind the head.

Draw a head with eyes, nose, mouth, and ear. Work chunky, short spiky bangs across the head: you only want a few points.

Now create a spiky profile around the whole head, finishing just below the ear.

Indicate an area of highlight behind the bangs, across the top of the head.

Ink around the outline of the hair, then ink the spikes of the bangs. Take this ink line up to the jagged edge of the highlight.

Next outline the area of highlight, around the crown and across the spiky front.

Color your hairstyle jet black. Work up to the highlight you outlined. Leave a couple of white areas so that the spikes of the bangs are seen as separate from the hair.

SLEEKY AND BLUE

This is a much more conservative, almost somber hairstyle. It falls down in straight lines from the center part, cut around the ears and ending in a razor-sharp line at the bottom. The style suggests a serious, straightforward personality.

Create a basic head with eyes, nose, mouth, and ear. Start the hairstyle by adding a center part; continue this beyond the top of the head.

From the part line, add hair falling down to shoulder level. Make the front of the style a cupid's bow and draw the locks down in front of the ear.

Work a jagged highlight near the top of the head, on one side only.

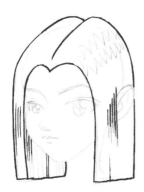

Start inking. Work from the cupid's bow down to the tips, and from the part down. Ink a few vertical lines in front of the ear, and on the left.

Ink the outline of the highlight on the right. This will be left white in the finished sketch.

Color the hair using an ice blue. Then take a darker blue and color to the left of the part, the underside of the hair on the left, below the ear, and on the tips of the hair on the right.

CROPPED RED BOB

This style is for a neat, modern girl with a fast-paced lifestyle, who needs a manageable tidy hairstyle that takes little maintenance. It is brushed forward around and under the ears, and has a side-swept full bangs. The bright red color makes it a very noticeable cut, but it would be easy to tone it down for a more reserved character.

Draw a basic head, with eyes, nose, mouth, and one ear. Create a large profile from the left eye over to the ear.

Now work a long spiky bangs across the face. Then add hair to the back of the head and down below the ear. Add a couple of spikes to this length on the left.

Create a broad spiky highlight across the top of the head.

Ink right around the outline of the hair in black.

Then, using red, ink the outline of the highlight across the top of the head.

Leaving the highlight white, color the rest of the hair bright red. Then create some darker red tips on the bangs.

CURLY STRANDS

Here is a slightly fussy head of curling strands, which fall down either side of the face and down the back of the head. It's a very feminine, rather old-fashioned style which would possibly suit a period story. The highlights give it a slightly more up-to-date feel, which could be exaggerated through using different colors.

Draw a basic head with eyes, nose, mouth, and one ear. From a point on top of the head create a piece of hair, that finishes in a spiky bangs.

From the top of the head, draw up and then down to shoulder level, creating a flick up. Add an oval next to where you started this piece.

Add a lock of hair in front of the ear, flicking this in. Complement this with a similar lock on the left, again flicking this in. Draw a spiky line behind the bangs.

Start inking by outlining all the top of the hair, from the part. Then ink the bangs and the curling locks flowing down.

Ink the spiky line that will form the edge of the highlight. Create spiky outlines of more highlights, two on each side of the face.

Color the hair dramatic black, leaving the highlights white.

GALLERY

happy

right This is a happy character: her smiling eyes and broad grin need a simple style to emphasize her personality.

golden shock

above A classic, blonde, spiky style, this complements the guileless blue eyes well. Use a darker shade of gold for shadows under the bangs.

samurai

above This unusual, rather severe style has a hard and shiny appearance, with overtones of a traditional samurai helmet.

feisty

left Here is a short, rather boyish style with punky spikes. It suggests that the character has a cute, feisty attitude.

innocent

above Pigtails can be used to make your character look young and innocent, but with a sense of fun. Bright green suggests a cheerful nature.

outgoing

above A standard ponytail in a bright color, this style gives a character a happy, confident, and outgoing personality.

cute

above A style like this one suits younger, girlie characters. The ribbon to complement the large loose ponytail is a good touch.

glamourous

above Suitable for slightly older females with sophistication, this style is soft and feminine, with a touch of glamour.

devious

above Long, dark hair and pointy ears suggest a devious nature, a characteristic emphasized by the narrow eyes and lopsided grin.

SHORT CROP

Sometimes the most effective haircut can be the most simple. Here is a standard crop, very popular with trendy young males and also tough guys and gangsters. It's a simple shape following the contours of the hairline, and can be filled predominantly with black, but with a slight area of color if needed.

Create a basic head with two eyes, nose, mouth, and one ear. Draw a wavy line to indicate the front of the hairline.

From the end of the wavy line draw around the top of the head, down and along the ear, creating sideburn, then work up to join the wavy line.

You have now created the basic outline of the hair, so ink over it.

Draw a wavy line on the top of the head, to create a highlight, then ink the rest of the hair using black.

To finish, color the highlight on top of the head using gray.

SIDE PART

This is a casual style for an everyday manga male. A loose cut parted on one side, and hanging down behind the ears to the collar. This type of style is suitable for a range of characters, and has a cool, confident look about it.

Draw a basic head, with two eyes, nose, mouth, and an ear. Starting higher than the outline of the head, work a few long spiky lines across your head.

Now complete the outline of the hair. Start from the starting point above the head and work up and round, creating spikes as you go. Finish with a couple of spikes in front of the ear.

Create a couple of spiky strands on the right on the face, to complete the profile of the hair.

Start to ink, working all around the profile of the hair. Ink a couple of lines on top of the head to help with shape.

Define an area of highlight across the top of the head using a gray pen.

Leaving the highlight white, color the rest of the hair gray.

BLUE AND SPIKY

Here we have a more fashionable look, with a variety of spikes and strands going off in various directions. Spiky hair is a typical manga look, often in bright, vivid colors. This style is in a bold blue, and is cut long at the sides in a contemporary fashion. Practice in creating spiky styles is always worth it.

Start by drawing a basic head, with two eyes, nose, mouth, and one ear. Then, starting outside the head, draw some long, spiky points of hair across the face.

Add a couple of long points of hair in front of the ear. Then, again starting outside the head area, draw a couple of similar length points on the right.

From same point as last time, work around the head, creating the profile of the hair. Echo the shape of the head, adding a couple of spikes on top.

Starting from where you made your first mark, ink the outline of the hair. Ink behind the bangs on the left-hand side so that the bangs looks right.

Create an area of highlight across the top of the head using a fine blue pen.

Color the hair blue. As a finishing touch, indicate a couple of stray strands of hair across the highlight, using a fine pen.

RED WARRIOR PONYTAIL

Old-fashioned styles like this are used in more traditional manga stories of sword fighters and samurai warriors. The hair is worn long at the back, with lengthy bangs and sides. Some of the hair is collected up in a high topknot, which sits upright from the top of the head, before cascading down the back. It's a dramatic, bold style and is very effective in portraying fast movement.

Draw a basic head, with eyes, nose, mouth, and one ear. In front of the ear, add some long, thin strands of hair.

Starting at the crown, draw a line out to the side and down, and use this to start drawing a spiky bangs to join your first long strands.

From the same start point, work a line over the crown and then create strands of hair behind the ear.

Now add a ponytail to the top of the head, held in place by a scrunchie. Take the ponytail to the same length as your longest spiked locks.

Ink around all the main lines of the hair, including all the spikes, the bangs and ponytail, and the scrunchie.

Create the outlines for two areas of highlight, one on top of the head, and one on the ponytail. Draw these using a fine red pen.

Leaving the highlights and the scrunchie white, color the hair bright red. Then color the underside of the ponytail and the tips of the hair with a darker shade of red.

FALLING BANGS

Large curtains like this are very popular in manga. This style is created from a basic center part, shoulder-length at the back, and brushed up into two dramatic bangs falling down on either side of the face. These are usually given shiny highlights to make them more emphatic and exaggerated.

Start by drawing a basic head, with eyes, nose, mouth, and one ear. Then draw the shape of a bird in flight, with the center line of your head at its center.

From each end of this line, draw a long curtain of spiky hair. Starting from the center line, draw jagged lines to meet the spiky curtains.

Next create the top of the hair, following the line of the top of the head, then draw some long strands down the back of the head on both sides.

Begin inking your hairstyle. Outline all the spikes and over the top of the head. Add a few wispy strands of hair from the center part.

Next create some areas of highlight on the spiky curtains of hair using a red-brown pen. Add one near the top and one in the middle of each.

Working around the white highlights, color your hairstyle reddish brown.

BLACK AND WHITE FASHIONISTA

Hairstyles can be very bold and creative in manga. This style is typical of a very fashionable youth-look, with asymmetrical spikes and a bold slash of white on the bangs. In what is essentially a black and white graphic medium, hairstyles like this are a useful way of making a character instantly identifiable.

Draw a basic head with eyes, nose, mouth, and one ear. Starting at the crown of the head, draw a curved line out and down, then four broad spikes, with a straight line back to the crown.

Starting about halfway down your last line, draw a spiky point over the left eye, then some longer spikes in front of the ear.

Add three large spikes on the crown, then draw down the back of the head behind the ear. Add a couple of horizontal spikes under the ear.

Ink all the main lines of the sketch. Make sure that the top area that you created first, on top of the head, reads as separate from the rest of the hairstyle.

Now start to color. Create some zigzags on the spikes on the left, and leave the area below white for now. Also leave the top area white. Color everything else black.

Color the spikes a dark gray, then add some touches of pale gray to the tips of the white hair.

BLACK PONYTAIL

This is a simple-looking ponytail, bunched at the back of the head. The cut is a basic, unremarkable style, and would probably suit a character unconcerned with fashion and trends, perhaps somebody from a rural background. The white highlight around the crown helps to emphasize the round shape of the haircut.

Draw a basic head with eyes, nose, mouth, and ear. Then, starting at the ear, draw spiky bangs. Continue the bangs well outside the head.

Starting where your last line finished, draw around the top of the head, adding three spikes at the crown, and continue your line down to the top of the ear.

Add a ponytail with a curly, flicked-up end flowing out behind the ear. Then indicate a spiky area of highlight on top of the head.

Now, using black, color your hairstyle. Leave the highlight you penciled white, coloring the top of the head. Leave some white flashes on the ponytail, then color it.

Ink around the profile of the hair, including the ponytail.

WILD PINK SPIKES

Here is a bold spiky look for a passionate, young male character. The spikes are jutting out in all directions like a flaming fire, and the color is eye-catching and dramatic. The style would suggest a fiery, passionate temperament.

Create a basic head with eyes, nose, mouth, and an ear. Starting in front of the ear, work across drawing a series of spikes for bangs. Continue this outside the area of the head.

Then, starting where you finished, work more large spikes right around the head, behind the ear, and down into the side of the neck.

Now draw a spiky halo on top of the head, within the outer ring of spikes. Sit some on the crown, and bring some into the spikes of the bangs. Add a few spikes in between those on the top of the head.

Ink around both haloes of spikes. Then ink around the spikes you interspersed between those on top of the head.

Finally color your hairstyle a dramatic dark pink color. Where the top halo casts shadows on the rest of the hair, double up on color, or use a darker purple.

SIMPLE BLONDE

This is a neat, simple haircut for a nice, sensible character. It suggests honesty and openness, and could be used for a college student or sports star perhaps. It has a basic center part, and is cut to a loose collar-length at the back.

Create a basic head with eyes, nose, mouth, and one ear. Draw a center line from crown to forehead, then flick lines to the left and to the right.

Add a couple of lines on top of the ear. Then make a series of spikes between your single line and the ear. From the two lines draw down a few spikes of hair.

Start on the right, and create the top of the hair to the center line, then work down behind the ear, and draw three spikes beside the neck. Add a few lines on the right.

Ink the main lines of the hairstyle, including the center line so that the style reads as having a definite center part.

Now start to add color. Use a bright yellow for the top left area, then use a more golden tone for the top right and down the left-hand side. Color the spiky area on the right using brown.

GREEN MOHAWK

Punk styles are familiar to manga readers, and this is a good example of a striking cut that can make a character stand out from the crowd. The Mohawk is derived from Native Americans, but has become a fashion classic with the alternative youth cultures of the last few decades.

Draw a basic head with eyes, nose, mouth, and an ear. Start with a center line, then draw a series of upright lines from the middle of the hairline.

Create the profile of the Mohawk from the top of the uprights to the back of the head.

Add groups of three lines, working back along the center line. Note that the lines get shorter as you near the back of the head.

Ink all the main lines. Start with the outline of the Mohawk, then ink all the upright lines.

Finally use two shades of green to color your hairstyle. Use a paler color in between the inked uprights, and a darker shade for the front of the Mohawk to give it width.

RED SWEPT-BACK

Not all manga hair has to fall down in front of the face. Here is a style swept up from the forehead in fiery red waves. It's cut high and short at the back to focus attention on the top, and a glossy white highlight gives dramatic visual impact.

Start by drawing a basic head with eyes, nose, mouth, and one ear. Then, starting from the ear, draw a series of short spikes across the forehead to indicate the hairline.

Next, starting where you finished, draw a series of large spikes over the top of the head, and down to the ear.

Now draw the outline of a highlight right across the top of the head.

Ink around the entire outline of the hairstyle.

Leaving the highlight white, color the hair bright red. Then add some darker red shadows on the points of the bangs, on the large spike behind the ear, and the hair in front of the ear.

PAGEBOY WITH BANGS

A traditional feudal-era style, this pageboy cut would be suitable for stories set in a bygone age. It's feminine by today's standards but very much a male cut in its own time. The highlights on the main hair body and the part, give a healthy-looking sheen.

Draw a basic head with eyes, nose, mouth, and one ear. Starting from the ear, draw a line up and across the head, just above eye level. Continue it out beyond the line of the head.

From where you finished, draw the profile of the hairstyle, making it high and smooth. Take it down below the ear, and smooth into the neck. Add a similar piece on the right.

Next, chop the bangs into thick, fairly even chunks. Then outline a highlight across the top of the head. Make some of the highlight cut across the bangs.

Ink around the basic shape of the hairstyle, then ink around the highlight. Where this cuts across the bangs, do not ink so that the gaps remain in the bangs. Add a couple of inked lines in the highlight.

Finally, working around the outlined highlight and creating another one on the right of the part, color the hair black.

GALLERY

frustrated

above Dramatic spikes in subdued colors suggest frustration, a look complemented by this boy's drawn brow, grimacing mouth, and strong shadows on the face and hair.

furious

below Red hair always points to a fiery temperament and a hint of danger. This character is in a fight, with his wide open mouth suggesting a yell of defiance.

dejected

above The dark hair here complements the dark eyes, with rings under them. His skin tone is washed out too: this character clearly has had a bad day.

innocent

left Wide eyes with close pupils and a shock of blue hair point to an innocent, happy character.

drenched

right The weather can do great things to hair. Here the rain has plastered it in streaks to the character's face.

sinister

below A shock of crown hair lit from below, together with the large eyes, point to a rather sinister character.

handsome youth

right This is a great look for a bishounen male: these characters are always slightly effeminate with fashionable hair and clothes.

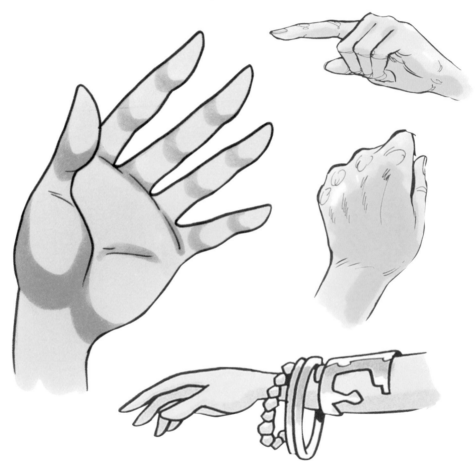

Hands And Arms

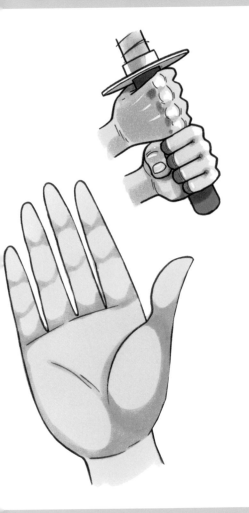

From a pointing finger to a clenched fist, hands are a very expressive part of a character. They can be tricky to get right. Looking at your own hands is important: practice flexing them and see how the joints work and how the fingers and thumb bend in relation to each other. This chapter covers a wide range of useful hand poses.

PROFILE HAND

Here is a basic hand in profile, with thumb and fingers all extended in a gentle curving pose. This hand shows the basic distance between the ball of the thumb and the back of the hand, and the relative length of the fingers. It could be reaching out to hold something, or waving.

Start by drawing an eggcup shape, and add a curved line to close it across the top. Next draw two lines coming down for the wrist, and add a short center line parallel to them.

Draw two ovals, one for the pad and one for the top of the thumb, and join with a curved line. Then draw two circles on the opposite side of the palm, and join with curved lines.

Now flesh out the thumb and first finger by joining the ovals and circles you have made.

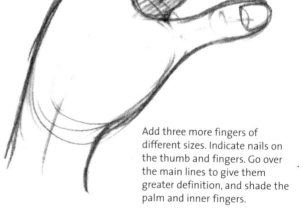

Add three more fingers of different sizes. Indicate nails on the thumb and fingers. Go over the main lines to give them greater definition, and shade the palm and inner fingers.

OPEN HAND

This is a standard open-palm view with all fingers extended and parallel to each other. It shows clearly the basic shapes of the hand, and is a good starting point. You can see how the ball of the thumb takes up one side of the palm, with a similar shape on the opposite side. There is also a distinct line where the fingers begin. Each finger is clearly divided into three segments.

Draw an eggcup shape for the palm and close its top with a curved line. Bisect it vertically with a line, and add two curved lines to indicate the wrist.

Take a slightly curved line out to the right. Draw a curved line into the palm and about two-thirds up your thumb line. Add a small semicircle next to this.

Draw two fingers on either side of your center line. Keep them in the correct proportion with one another and give each two joints. Use your own hand for reference.

Ink around the outside of the hand and add creases on the palm, across the wrist, and at the base of the fingers. Color your hand pink.

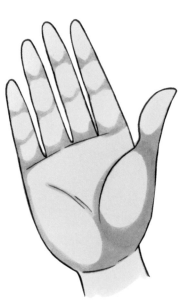

Start to build up areas of shadow using orange-brown. Shadows form around the joints, at the base of the palm and along its creases, and up into the thumb.

TENSE HAND

You can see here how the finger joints operate. Beginning with the knuckles, each joint folds in on itself until the hand becomes a closed ball. The fingers here are not clenched tightly enough to make a fist, but show a degree of tension.

Start with an eggcup shape, with one side longer than the other. Close the top with a curved line. Add a center line at the base of the palm, and lines for the wrist.

Draw four circles across your top line: these will be the knuckle joints. Now add a line from each circle to give you the outer line of each finger.

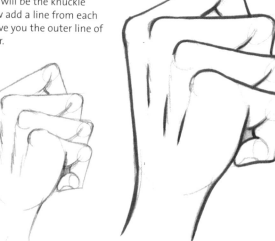

Add an ellipse to the end of each line and use these to position the first joint of each finger. Add a second joint to the finger closest to you.

Refine the main lines of your hand and fingers, and add a nail to the closest finger. Then indicate the creases on the back of the hand.

Ink in all your main lines, around the wrist, palm, and all the fingers. Ink the creases on the back of the hand and on the finger joints you can see.

HANGING LOOSE

Much of the time a character's hand may be seen hanging down loosely by his or her side. This is shown as a relaxed downward-pointing profile shape, as here. The fingers can be seen to curl slightly inward, leading away from the index finger: having them all pointing straight down would look unnatural.

Draw an egg shape. At its top, add two lines to indicate the wrist. Add a center line here, break it, then pick it up and continue out of the bottom of the egg.

Butt an oval up to this line, about halfway along it. Join this to the egg shape with a short line, then add a curved line to flesh out shape of the thumb.

Draw a line from the left of the egg, down parallel to, and closing in on the first. This is the index finger. Then add the top joints for the three other fingers.

Ink around the edges of the wrist, palm, fingers, and thumb, so that they all are clearly separate from one another. Then erase your pencil lines.

Color the whole of the drawing pink. Make the color solid at this stage: you will be adding shading to indicate shaping and molding at the next stage.

Use tan to add shape to the hand. The areas in shadow are on the right of the wrist and thumb, the right of the index finger, and around the joints.

CLENCHED FIST

A very useful pose, particularly in action manga, is the closed fist. Here you can see a view looking down on the back of the hand, and you can see clearly the tensed-up sinews that connect the muscle to the bone. The knuckles are clearly indicated at the top of the shape.

Draw an eggcup shape at a 45° angle. Then draw two lines down from it to make a wrist. Close off the top with a curved line, then sketch in a center line up from the wrist.

Create basic shapes for the knuckles by drawing four circles. Make the middle two butt up against the curved line; the first and last should sit across it.

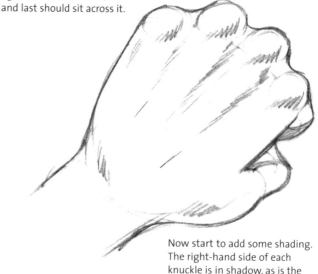

Define the thumb with two semicircles and a triangle, then create two joints for the index finger. Then outline around the whole hand.

Now start to add some shading. The right-hand side of each knuckle is in shadow, as is the base of the thumb. There is also shading around the wrist area.

CLAWING HAND

The hand is a tool that can be used for many different purposes. This is a clutching pose which is good for gripping, climbing, holding, and similar purposes. The index finger and the thumb are the principal levers, with the remaining fingers used for added grip. You can see how the fingers are folded at the joints, indicated by the darker tones.

Draw a U-shape and close off the top with a curved line. Add verticals top and bottom, then draw two short lines to create the wrist.

Add an oval, overlapping the right-hand edge of the palm, the whole length of the palm. Add the top joint of the thumb across the oval.

Draw the outer edge of the index finger, then create the fingers from a series of ovals and U shapes, butting to this line.

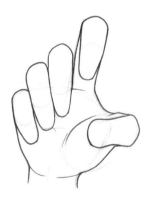

Ink around the edge of the hand, and around the individual fingers and thumb. Add ink, too, to the base of the thumb, the base of the first finger, and the wrist.

Now add a flat color over the whole hand. In this case, a pale pink was used.

Add some shading to those areas that are in shadow. These include the base of the hand, the tops of the fingers, the base of the index finger, and parts of the thumb.

PUNCHING FIST

This is a more dramatic view of a fist, which is coming towards the viewer. It shows how compact and tightly closed the fingers are, with the thumb tucked underneath to prevent any damage. You can see the shading indicating the knuckles across the top of the shape.

Begin by drawing a rectangle with one end smaller than the other and a curved upperside. The top line will become the line of the knuckles.

Draw three lines up from the bottom, stopping about three-quarters of the way up. Fill the gaps between them with a series of four ellipses.

Add an oval shape to the bottom right-hand corner, then sketch the last joint of the thumb which folds over the oval. Round off the bases of the fingers.

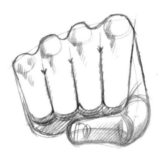

Redefine the main lines, creating definite gaps between the fingers and shadow at their bases. Then indicate shading on the palm and add a thumbnail.

Now ink the sketch. Ink around the outside of the hand, then ink the gaps between the fingers and the finger joints. Finally, ink around the thumbnail.

WAVING OPEN HAND

Here is a graceful, waving hand pose. The look is more feminine and flowing, with slender fingers and smooth lines. Female and male hands follow the same basic construction rules, but those of females can be smaller and smoother.

Draw an eggcup shape at an angle of 45°, then close off its top with a curved line. Add a curved line to bisect the basic shape and continue this out and up.

Create the base of the thumb by drawing an oval across the center line and out to the palm edge. Continue the wrist line up and back to create the thumb.

Draw down from your center line and up and down again to create the first and second fingers. Add the other two fingers. Then create joints on them.

Ink around the whole hand and the individual fingers. Define the edge of the thumb joint across the palm, and ink the crease at the base of each finger.

Now add a flat color to the hand. In this case a pale pink was used.

Create areas of shadow using a tan color. These include around the joints, across the palm, around the base of the thumb, and at the base of the hand.

BECKONING ARM

Once you have a grasp of hand construction, you can look at how the arm becomes involved. Here is a good pose, with a bended elbow and hand raised up to the shoulder level. It could be used to indicate a summons.

Draw three ovals, in a triangular shape. Make the top left oval broader at the top. Join them together with straight lines, then add a horizontal line on the right.

Add four circles to the top of the left oval. Then add two lines the width of the oval: these are the joints of the fingers. Draw in four fingers and a thumb.

Now add flesh to the arm. Join the hand to the oval elbow joint, and the elbow to the oval shoulder joint. Add the shoulder and neck, and a line for the side.

Ink around shoulder, arm, and hand. Ink the gaps between the individual fingers, and between the index finger and thumb.

Now introduce some color. Here a flat pale pink was used to color the hand, arm, and shoulder.

Add shading to suggest the roundness of the arm. Shade under the arm, the outside of the upper and lower arm, the back of the hand, and the finger joints.

CONTROLLED DETERMINATION

The average arm falls down to just below the hip. The pose here shows an arm and clenched fist held down by the side in a manner that suggests the figure is controlling his emotions. The position of the hip and buttocks counterbalances the arm and the forward leaning stance.

Draw two circles. Add a large ellipse, then butt the base of a triangle to it. Connect the two circles and the ellipse, and the two circles and the triangle.

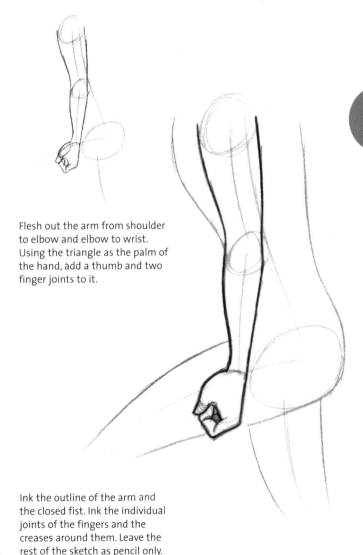

Flesh out the arm from shoulder to elbow and elbow to wrist. Using the triangle as the palm of the hand, add a thumb and two finger joints to it.

Add a suggestion of a body to which the arm is attached. The spine runs parallel to the arm down to the ellipse. One leg is straight, the other steps forward.

Ink the outline of the arm and the closed fist. Ink the individual joints of the fingers and the creases around them. Leave the rest of the sketch as pencil only.

WAVING ARM

An outstretched arm and hand can be used in a number of ways. Here, the fingers are spread as if to trying to grasp onto something, perhaps to stop the figure from falling. This sketch shows that even a fully outstretched arm is not entirely straight.

Draw two ovals, then a U-shape, closed with a curved line. Join these three shapes which are, from bottom to top, the shoulder joint, elbow joint, and hand.

Add an ellipse to the left of the hand for the thumb pad, and add a line coming from it for the thumb. Draw four ovals to create knuckles, then add the fingers.

Finish drawing the thumb, then flesh out the arm. Add a suggestion of a head, here half an ellipse with an ear shape, and add some spiky hair.

Ink around the arm and the individual fingers. Define the curve of the thumb on the palm, the life line, and the creases at the base of the fingers.

Add some flat color to the arm and hand. In this sketch, a pale pink was used.

Now add shading. Here the upper arm is in shadow, there is a hint of shadow along the right-hand side of the lower arm, and around the palm of the hand.

GRASPING AT YOU

This is a good dynamic action pose, where the hand is clutching toward the viewer with an arm bent at the elbow. It involves foreshortening, as the forearm is pointing horizontally toward you, rendering it as an oval shape behind the hand.

Slightly overlap two ovals, then draw a third a little distance away. This is the shoulder joint. Draw a line to attach this to one of the ovals: this is the foreshortened lower arm.

Draw four circles along the edge of oval: these are the first finger joints. Now create the two upper joints of each finger, these are roughly equal in length when viewed from this angle.

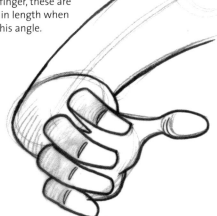

Add an ellipse to create the pad of the thumb, and join this to the hand with two curved lines.

Ink the main lines, including the creases around the top joint of each finger and under the pad of the thumb.

POINTING FINGER

A pointing hand can be very useful in a manga story. Here you can see how the index finger is stretched out in a straight line, with the remaining fingers folded back into the palm. The thumb is stretched out diagonally away from the hand in this case, although it can also be tucked away as in the fist pose.

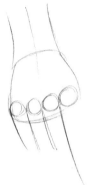

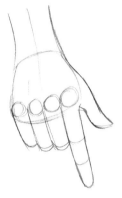

Draw an upside-down U-shape, closing off the open end with a curved line. This is the back of the hand. Add two lines for the wrist, and a center line.

Create the knuckles by drawing four circles across the back of the hand. Draw a short line at the side of the first three, with a longer one beside the fourth.

Join the three short lines with curved lines for the joints of the first three fingers. Add the pointing index finger with its joints, then add a thumb.

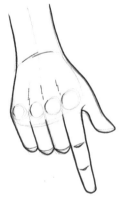

Ink around the main lines of the wrist, hand, fingers, and thumb. Add creases to the wrist and back of the hand, as well as to the knuckle and finger joints.

Leaving the knuckles white, add a flat color to the rest of the hand, fingers, and thumb.

Now create areas of shading. The left-hand side of the wrist is in shadow, as are the bent fingers, the left of the thumb, and the joints of the index finger.

GRIPPING HAND

A gripping hand can be applied to any object from a sword to a tennis racquet. The hand here is grasping a handle or hilt of some kind. The index finger is slightly extended beyond the rest of the fingers, which is a natural position and gives extra control. The tip of the thumb can be seen curving round behind the handle.

Draw two ellipses at right angles to each other. Bisect the larger with a circle, then add two more circles. Join the three circles with a curved line, and draw two straight lines, one each side of the smaller ellipse.

Then draw three circles outside the left-hand line and three bisecting the right hand line. Join these to make three finger joints.

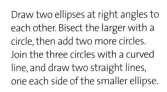

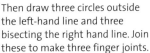

Create the index finger by fleshing out the first three circles you drew. Leave a gap between the index finger and the other three. Then add the thumb.

Ink around the wrist, hand, fingers, and thumb. Add some shading around the joints. To finish, strengthen the baton the hand is holding, adding shading.

FINGER ON THE TRIGGER

This pose shows how to hold the stock of a weapon while keeping a finger on the trigger. The important thing here is to visualize the weapon handle when you draw the hand, otherwise the grip will look unnatural. Note how the three remaining fingers fold down around the stock.

Draw an ellipse, and add two curved lines for a wrist. Draw four circles, one overlapping the ellipse, two inside it, and the last protruding only a little. Add a short line out from the top circle.

The four circles are knuckle joints. From the lower three, draw finger joints. From the line at the top, draw the rounded joint of the index finger. Draw the fold of skin between the two fingers.

Now get an indication of the weapon that the hand is holding. This has a base under the fingers, together with the trigger and a suggestion of the barrel. This does not need to be detailed.

Ink the hand to emphasize it. Ink around the wrist, sides, and individual fingers. Ink the joints, and define the knuckles.

Now add a flat color over the hand. In this sketch, a pale pink has been used.

Add some shading to those areas that need it. These are the underside of the wrist and hand, and the finger joints.

FOLDED ARMS

One of the hardest things to get right is a pair of folded arms. It can be a dramatic visual example of body language in a manga story, and makes a character look firm and immovable. You can see how the chest is arched backward slightly to exaggerate the gesture.

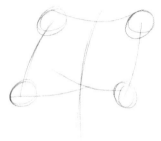

Create shoulder and elbow joints by drawing four circles, one at each corner of an imaginary square. Join the top three with straight lines, and add a center line. Draw a line from each elbow across the chest.

Flesh out the upper and lower arms by joining the joints. The lower arms are folded so draw one on top of the other. Indicate a torso.

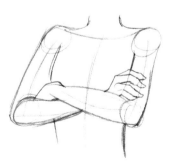

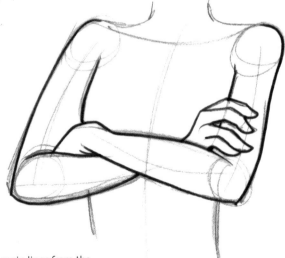

Add shoulders and a suggestion of a neck. Then work on the hands. The left hand has no detail. Add four jointed fingers to the right hand, above the elbow.

Ink the main lines from the shoulders, down the arms, and around the individual fingers.

135

GALLERY

pointing

right The index finger points and the rest of the fingers are folded. The tip of the thumb peeps out.

gripping thumb

below With a thick accessory like a book, the thumb joint comes to the forefront. Only part of the palm and first finger are visible in this type of grip.

spread fingers

below This is a good neutral pose. Note that the shadows are on the right of the hand, in between the fingers, and to the right of all the knuckle joints.

holding

above In a holding pose, the thumb disappears, the index finger sticks out, and the knuckles form a sloping line.

semi-open

above In this pose, the fingers point, but in a far less aggressive manner than in other poses. The hand here is also more relaxed.

fingertip hold

below Finger and thumb come together to hold a fine item like a drinking straw. Take care with details such as the fingernails.

gripping fist

above When the fist is tightly closed around a staff or other weapon, the knuckles are prominent. A small area of thumb shows.

sword fight

right A closed-fist grip is used to hold weapons. Whoosh lines give the sensation of speed to static objects like swords.

two-fisted

below Action manga can involve holding all kinds of weapons. The hands are gripping tightly, giving strong highlights on the knuckles and dark shadows under the folded fingers.

punching

above This fist is pushing upward. Strong, dynamic coloring produces dark shadows and bright highlights.

S

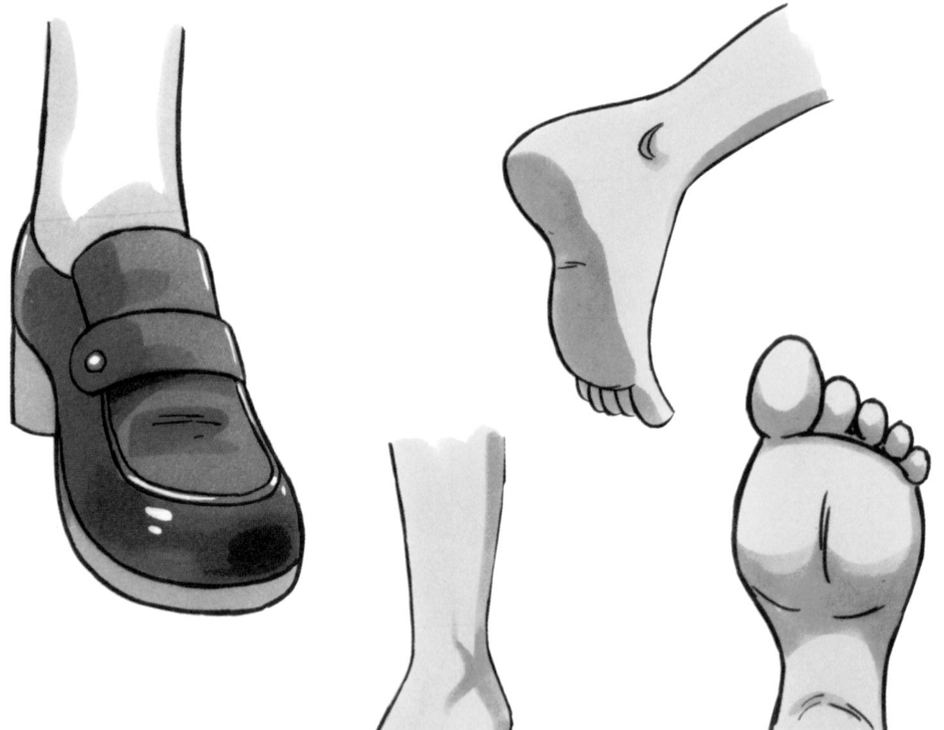

Legs And Feet

Bare, booted, or clad in athletic shoes, feet can add a great deal to your characters' believability. Like hands, feet can be difficult to get right. Most feet have some sort of footwear, nevertheless an understanding of the basic anatomy of the foot is a must. This chapter takes a variety of foot positions and shoe types to get you started.

PROFILE FOOT

This is probably the easiest view of the foot to draw. It shows the angle of the heel as it juts out from the leg, as well as the smooth curve of the instep leading down to the toes. This foot is pointing down as if about to step, so the weight would be on the ball of the foot.

Start with a small oval shape at the bottom, then draw a larger rounded triangle shape above for the heel. Draw a vertical line down for the leg, then connect the two shapes with an arc, and a short upward curve for the toes.

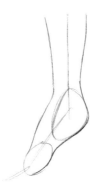

Flesh out the leg shape, working the calf and then the foot. Leave the line for the toe at this point.

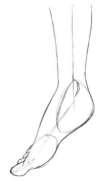

Now add the toes. Start with the big toe, then create smaller curves for the rest of the toes.

Ink around the outline of the leg, defining the separate toes. Add a nail to the big toe.

Now add a flat tint color over the whole drawing. In this case, pale pink was used.

Create some modeling using dark beige. There is shading down the back of the leg, around the ankle, and under the foot.

TOP OF THE FOOT

This view shows the basic shape of the foot looking down from above. You can see the spread of the toes and the angle in relation to the leg. This foot has a fairly solid contour, suggesting a male, whereas a female foot would usually be more slender width at the ankle.

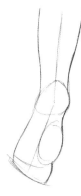

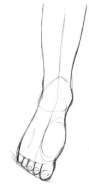

Start with a rounded triangle for the ankle joint. Add a straight line for the leg and another for the foot. Indicate the toes with a curved line at this stage.

Add an ellipse for the pad of the foot, then flesh out the shape of the leg and the foot. Add a curved line to indicate the base of the toes.

Now flesh out the individual toes and give the first three toenails; toenails will not "read" on the smallest two toes.

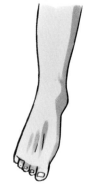

Ink around the whole drawing, separating the toes and inking the nails. Add a couple of lines to suggest the bulge of the instep.

Now color your illustration using a flat pale pink.

Suggest modeling using a dark beige. There is shading to the right of the leg, along the right-hand side of the foot, and around the instep.

KICKING OUT

Here is a good view of the foot as it kicks out behind a figure in a sharp arc. It could be delivering a blow from a martial artist or be the trailing foot of a diving or flying figure. Note how the foot is pulled back sharply, forming a smooth continuous line from the leg.

Draw a triangle with rounded edges to represent the heel joint. Bisect this with a straight line for the foot, and a slightly curved one for the toe line.

Flesh out the basic shape of the leg and foot.

Now add the toes, with toenails. Indicate the ankle joint by drawing a small triangle.

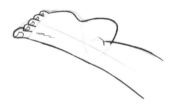

Ink the main lines of the sketch. This includes the leg, heel, ankle joint, and toes and toenails. Suggest the line of the instep.

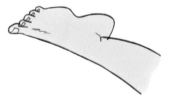

Color your sketch. Here a flat pale pink was used.

Use a dark beige to get some shading and modeling into your foot. There is shading on the left-hand side of the leg and foot, and across the toes.

STEPPING OFF

In this drawing, the foot is lifted as if stepping off to the right. It is tilted slightly away from the viewer so you can clearly see the sole and the undersides of the toes. From the heel to the ball of the foot there is an arch which indents in a smooth curve, and you can see the heel is narrower than the ball.

Start by drawing a rounded triangle for the heel, then add a straight diagonal line up to the right for the leg, and a two-part line down to the bottom right for the foot.

Flesh out the leg and the ball of the foot, with a suggestion of the big toe.

Draw an ellipse for the ball of the foot, then flesh this out into the heel. Draw in the toes.

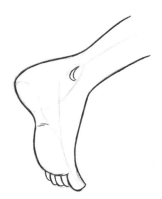

Ink the outline of the leg and foot, including the toes. Ink, too, an indication of the ankle joint and the edge of the footpad.

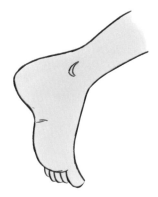

Color your whole sketch. Here a flat pale pink was used.

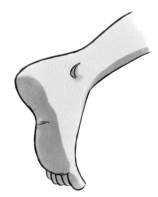

Add shading to refine the shape of the leg and foot. Most of the underside of the foot is in shadow, as is an area on the front of the leg and around the ankle joint.

THREE-QUARTER VIEW

From another angle, you can see how the toes are used to balance the weight of the foot, and how the arch is used to direct the movement of the tread. The ankle here is sharply defined with strong shadows.

Draw a triangle with rounded sides, then a straight line to represent the leg. At this stage, make three lines for the foot.

Flesh out the leg and foot. Draw verticals up from the triangle to make the leg. Then draw from the triangle down to make the foot. Block in the line of the toes.

Create the ankle joint, then add the toes. Indicate toenails.

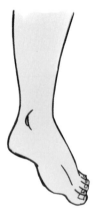

Ink the outline of the leg and foot. Then ink the ankle joint and the line of the instep. Ink the toes separately, then ink the individual toenails.

Color the leg and foot; here a flat pale pink was used.

Then introduce shading and modeling, using a dark beige, on the left of the leg, around the ankle, and under the foot.

STEPPING LEG

Now try drawing this leg, which is bent slightly at the knee in a forward stepping position, with the foot flat on the floor and ready to take the weight of the body as it moves forward. Note how the shin is relatively flat while the calf behind curves out to contain the muscle.

Start by drawing basic shapes: an ellipse for the knee joint and a wedge for the foot. Draw a line from the apex of the triangle to the center of the ellipse, and another from the top of the ellipse up.

Now flesh out the leg. Add two lines down to the knee to create the thigh, then work down, tapering in to the ankle.

Start to add more detail. Redefine the kneecap. Then, refine the foot, giving it a clear profile and outlining the big toe. Draw a triangle to suggest the ankle bone.

Ink the outline of the leg and foot. Then ink the kneecap and ankle bone. Finally, suggest some of the other toes.

Now get some color into your sketch. In this case, a flat pale pink was used.

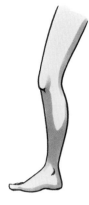

Finally use a dark beige for modeling and shading. There is shading down the back of the leg and on the shin, around the kneecap, and under the foot.

145

GALLERY

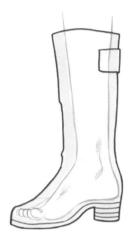

athletic shoe

left Street characters as well as sporting figures need athletic shoes. Personalize through use of color.

high-heeled boot

above Always visualize the shape of the foot inside a shoe or boot. This high-heeled style is suitable for many different types of character.

sturdy boot

left Chunky all-purpose boots are a must in all kinds of situations, They can be sturdy like these or more dainty to give a cuter look.

inline skate

right Sports footwear adds interest to lots of characters, and works for girls and boys.

high-front boot

right This is a standard style of boot given an upbeat twist through the use of two shades of green in the coloring.

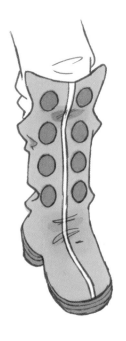

heavyweight boot

above This chunky-looking boot is suitable for street-fighters and space-walkers alike.

sandal

above Greek-style sandals are ideal for more surreal characters, and relatively easy to draw.

pointed boot

right This is a good boot for lots of different characters. Vary the number of buckles and the height of the heel to create lots of different looks.

winged boot

above A side wing is a good finishing touch to a standard boot; this short, slim model has a high heel.

SOLE OF THE FOOT

To understand the structure of the foot, it's a good idea to study the sole and see how the various parts relate to each other. Here you can see clearly the different widths of the ball and heel, and the descending position and size of the toes.

Draw an egg shape to represent the heel and an irregular ellipse for the ball of the foot. Join them with a curved line.

Join the two basic shapes to create the profile of the sole.

Now add the toes along the curved line that forms the top of the foot: the big toe is an ellipse, the others are rounder.

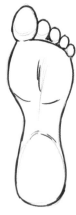

Ink the main lines of your sketch. Ink the outline of the foot as well as the individual toes. Ink a suggestion of the ball of the foot and the heelpad.

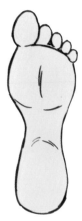

Color the entire foot using a flat pale pink.

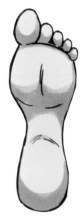

Now get some shading into the foot. The bases of the toes are in shadow, as is the area of the arch and part of the heelpad.

STANDING LEG, FRONT VIEW

From the front, the leg is a much narrower shape. It should taper in at the knee and again at the ankle before spreading out at the foot. Note how that kneecap sits centrally about halfway up the leg, and protrudes from the middle.

Draw a rough circle for a kneecap, with a triangle with a curved base for a foot. Add two verticals for the leg.

Now flesh out the leg. Add a line going into the knee, out again for the calf, and tapering into the ankle on both sides of the leg.

Redefine the kneecap, then work on the foot. Draw circles for the toes, and define the profile of the sole.

Ink the outline of the leg, defining the ankle, heel, and toes. Ink the kneecap, and add a couple of lines for the front of the ankle.

Now add color, here a flat pale pink has been used over the whole leg and foot.

Use shading to get some modeling into the leg. There are shadows down the left of the leg and under the knee at the front. Suggest shading on the toes.

RED ANKLE BOOT

Here's a funky little ankle boot with a cuff, which would look good in a fantasy or sci-fi story. It has a thick cushioned sole for comfort, and a white trim detail around the cuff. Note how the upper of the shoe is creased as the foot steps forward, which makes the material of the shoe look soft and pliable.

Draw a rounded triangle for the ankle joint. Add a vertical for the leg bone, a curve for the top of the foot, a line for the foot itself, and an upright for the line of the toes.

Get some body into the shoe. Make a thick sole, then put a couple of lines in to indicate the top of the shoe.

Now add the cuff, with an inverted V detail, and flesh out the leg.

Create the profile of the heel, add a trim detail to the cuff, and indicate a couple of creases in the top of the boot.

Ink all the main lines,
including the creases
you outlined in pencil.

Finally use dark red to
indicate shadows on
the boot, under the
cuff, on the cuff, and on
the sole. Use gray for
areas of shadow on the
welt and sole.

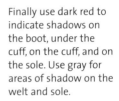

Color the leg pale pink,
then color the boot red.
Leave white the trim on
the cuff, the heel welt,
and the sole.

SCHOOL SHOE

Now we can draw a foot wearing a shoe. The shape of the shoe may vary but it should always be able to contain a realistic foot shape. This style is a typical school-type shoe, with sock, probably worn by a young female character. It has a strap-fastening across the top of the foot, and a broad rounded toe.

Start with a rough triangle and a rough rectangle, and join them together with straight lines.

Flesh out the foot by joining the triangle and rectangle, then indicate the bottom of a leg.

Draw the body of the shoe, with its crosspiece. Define the sole.

Create a couple of highlights, add a fastener to the shoe, then indicate a ribbed sock.

Ink your sketch. Then, color the shoe black, working around the highlight areas you defined. The shoe now has the appearance of shiny patent leather.

UTILITY BOOT

This is a robust-looking functional boot, with a practical flat sole and reinforced toe and heel parts. It would be suitable for a military uniform or for a motorcycle rider, and would suit either a male or female foot. The loose folds around the lip indicate that the trousers are tucked inside the boot.

Draw a circle for the knee and a triangle for the foot. Join these with a vertical and add another vertical for the upper leg.

Create the basic shape of the three-quarter boot.

Now add the trouser-covered leg, with fabric bunching around the knee and tucked into the boot.

Define the sole, heel guard, and toecap of the boot, and add some detailing to the top.

Build up some shading on the boot. Shade the sole and around the middle of the side to round out the shape, making the boot look more realistic.

TREKKING BOOT

Using a stepping-off foot position as a base, this sturdy walking boot has a firm toecap and six-eyehole laces. The sole has a deep functional tread, ideal for all-terrain exploring or simple urban streets. Note how the heel is deeper than the rest of the sole, which gives the foot extra support where it's needed.

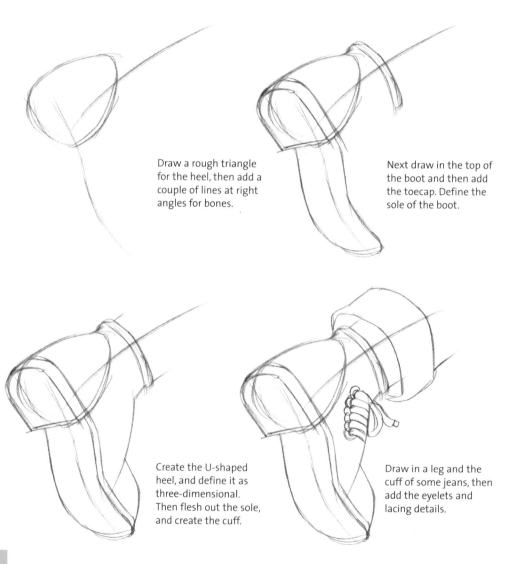

Draw a rough triangle for the heel, then add a couple of lines at right angles for bones.

Next draw in the top of the boot and then add the toecap. Define the sole of the boot.

Create the U-shaped heel, and define it as three-dimensional. Then flesh out the sole, and create the cuff.

Draw in a leg and the cuff of some jeans, then add the eyelets and lacing details.

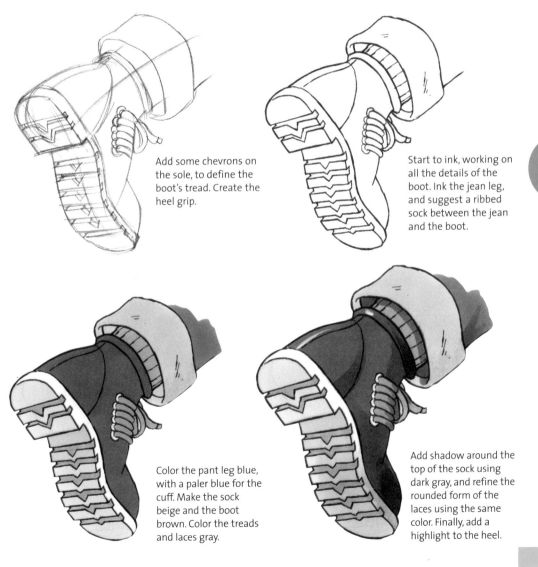

Add some chevrons on the sole, to define the boot's tread. Create the heel grip.

Start to ink, working on all the details of the boot. Ink the jean leg, and suggest a ribbed sock between the jean and the boot.

Color the pant leg blue, with a paler blue for the cuff. Make the sock beige and the boot brown. Color the treads and laces gray.

Add shadow around the top of the sock using dark gray, and refine the rounded form of the laces using the same color. Finally, add a highlight to the heel.

BALLET PUMP

This ballet pump is a very common everyday shoe worn by female manga characters. It sits snugly around the foot, and has a thin flat sole, comfortable for walking around town. Take care that the foot shape is established under the outline of the pump, to ensure an accurate and believable piece of footwear.

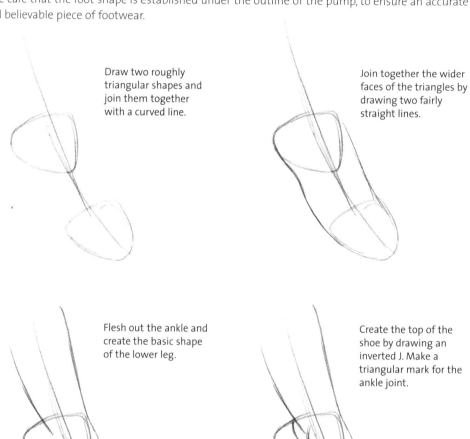

Draw two roughly triangular shapes and join them together with a curved line.

Join together the wider faces of the triangles by drawing two fairly straight lines.

Flesh out the ankle and create the basic shape of the lower leg.

Create the top of the shoe by drawing an inverted J. Make a triangular mark for the ankle joint.

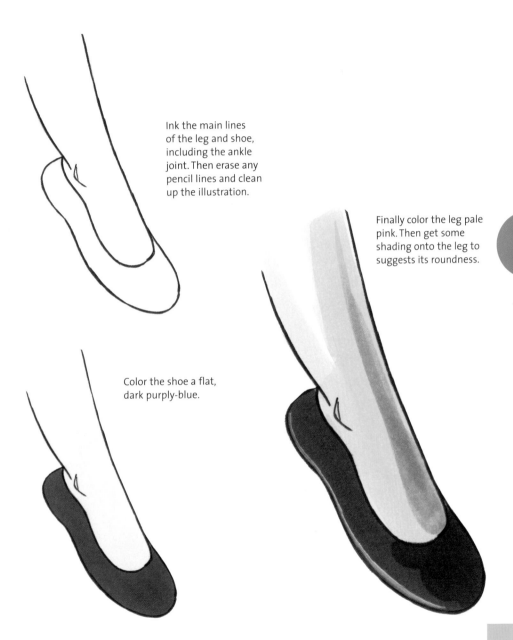

Ink the main lines of the leg and shoe, including the ankle joint. Then erase any pencil lines and clean up the illustration.

Finally color the leg pale pink. Then get some shading onto the leg to suggests its roundness.

Color the shoe a flat, dark purply-blue.

CHUNKY HEEL BOOT

Some female characters wear a higher-heel boot for extra lift. This style is a chunky, stack-heeled boot with a zip-up side and flat, wide toe. You can see how the heel curves round the back of the foot in a smooth line, then creases slightly as the calf bows outward again.

Draw a rough triangle, with a curved line cutting through it.

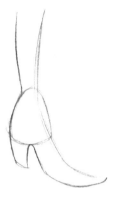

Draw a vertical roughly parallel to the first, then create the heel of the boot from the base of the triangle, and the profile of the front and sole.

Flesh out the rest of the boot, then redefine the sole, and create the third dimension for the heel.

Add some detailing at the side of the boot, create the detailing on the heel, and add shading here. Then create some creases on the front and around the ankle.

Ink the main lines, including the creases. Then use black to define the top of the boot and make the shading on the heel.

SENSIBLE LACE-UP

This is a typical shoe for a male businessman. It's a traditional-looking lace-up shoe with toe and heel areas clearly defined. The heel is slightly deeper than the main sole, but not by much. The laces are tied in two loops in the normal manner. It's well worth looking at a pair of real laces to help you to get this drawing correct.

Draw two roughly triangular shapes and join them together with an angled line.

Join the triangles together with a double line, to create the sole, then add a heel. Create the upper from a curved line.

Add the eyelets and then the laces, which are a series of parallel lines.

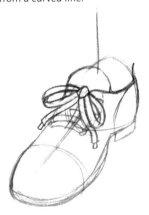

Sketch the heelguard, then create a bow for the lace.

Add a trouser leg and the suggestion of a ribbed sock. Create some shading on the pant leg, then on the upper of the shoe.

LEATHER SLIP-ON

This is another sensible-looking shoe, suitable for a young female office-worker or professional woman. It's made of smart brown leather with moccasin-style piping around the top, and a button-down strap-fastening across. The heel is quite high but still sensible-looking.

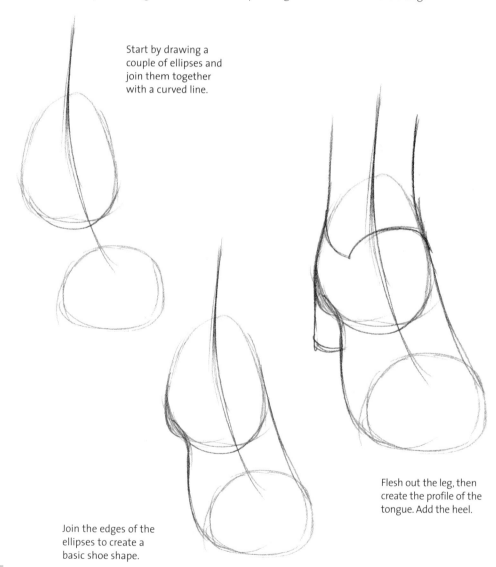

Start by drawing a couple of ellipses and join them together with a curved line.

Flesh out the leg, then create the profile of the tongue. Add the heel.

Join the edges of the ellipses to create a basic shoe shape.

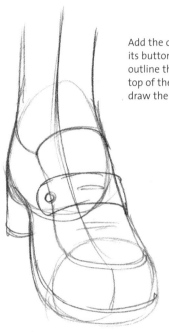

Add the crosspiece with its button detail, then outline the leather on the top of the shoe. Finally draw the sole.

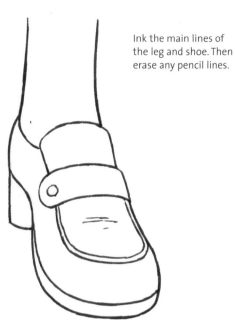

Ink the main lines of the leg and shoe. Then erase any pencil lines.

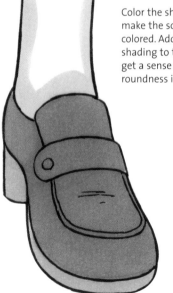

Color the shoe tan and make the sole honey-colored. Add some blue shading to the leg to get a sense of roundness into it.

Finally take some opaque white and use it to work some highlights on the upper and on the button detail.

Clothing

If you can dress your figures convincingly, you are well on the way to creating great manga. The outfits in this chapter vary from historical to futuristic, and from real life to fantasy. The best way to start drawing fabric, in particular, is to look at things around you, such as curtains and drapes, and note how their folds fall.

SMART SUIT

Every man must have a suit in his wardrobe. This manga male is wearing a typical two-piece suit and loafers. Note how the creases on each leg are clearly indicated, and how the jacket goes in at the waist to give a tailored look. The outfit is finished off with a folded handkerchief in the breast pocket.

Draw a basic figure using lines for bones, circles for joints, and triangles for pelvis and feet. Give him some hair. Add the top of a jacket, to waist level, then draw in the lapels. Add a collar and tie.

Add sleeves from the shoulders, down over the elbow joints. Add the rest of the jacket over the pelvis. Include patch pockets and a single button. Indicate creasing around the waist.

Next add trousers and shoes. Then finish off the figure's arms by adding hands.

Refine the lines of the collar and tie , then shade the tie. Add a handkerchief in the top pocket.

Ink all the main lines of your suit, shirt and tie, and shoes. Also ink the lines of the creases in the jacket and trousers.

MARTIAL ARTS

This is a typical martial arts suit, known as a karategi, or "gi" for short. It consists of a kimono top and dogi pants. The gi is loose-fitting to allow freedom of movement, and tied at the waist with a belt. The color of the belt denotes the grade, or skill-level. of the wearer. The character shown here has a black belt, which means he has achieved the highest grade of training (black belts themselves are further graded in levels known as first dan, second dan, third dan, and so on).

Start with a basic stick figure with lines for bones, circles for joints, and triangles for pelvis and feet. Draw the top of the jacket, down to the waist. Add the trim around the neck, and the belt at the waist.

Next, give him some baggy pants to just below knee level, then give your character legs and feet: there is no footwear in this costume.

Draw the rest of the jacket, then work on the details of the belt. Next draw the sleeves and give the figure hands. Draw in some creases at the elbows.

Now ink over the main lines, including the creases around the elbows, into the waist, and on the pants. Color the belt black, along with the insides of the sleeves and the shadow at the neckline.

STREET GEAR

For a cool-looking youth, try this bolero-length jacket and slim pants. The collar is worn up to convey attitude, and the shoulders are cut wide for a masculine feel. The white pants are slightly flared at the bottom, and have a narrow belt for contrast.

Next draw in the sleeves, with some creasing around the elbows, and add his hands. Indicate trim along the zipper and breast pockets.

Draw a basic stick figure with lines for bones, circles for joints, and triangles for pelvis and feet. Start with his bolero jacket, detailing the stand-up collar.

Add some trousers, with a flat waistband, then pocket details, and flared legs. Add his teeshirt, and give him shoes.

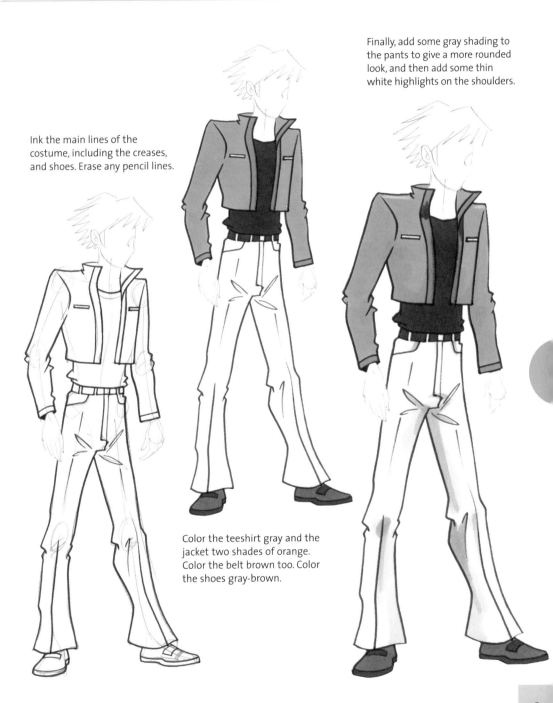

Finally, add some gray shading to the pants to give a more rounded look, and then add some thin white highlights on the shoulders.

Ink the main lines of the costume, including the creases, and shoes. Erase any pencil lines.

Color the teeshirt gray and the jacket two shades of orange. Color the belt brown too. Color the shoes gray-brown.

MILITARY GREATCOAT

Here's a much heavier look for a sci-fi or period story. The broad cuffs and collar have a military look, with a double-breasted front and a narrow belt at the waist. The boots are sturdy-looking and reinforced with steel. The yellow neckerchief gives a dashing touch of color to the coat, which is a drab, somber green.

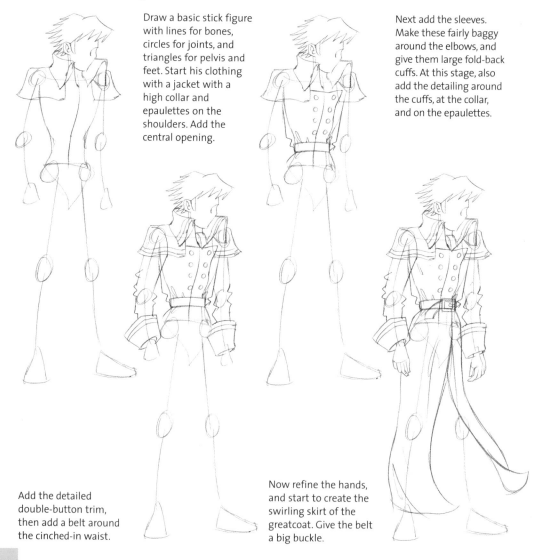

Draw a basic stick figure with lines for bones, circles for joints, and triangles for pelvis and feet. Start his clothing with a jacket with a high collar and epaulettes on the shoulders. Add the central opening.

Next add the sleeves. Make these fairly baggy around the elbows, and give them large fold-back cuffs. At this stage, also add the detailing around the cuffs, at the collar, and on the epaulettes.

Add the detailed double-button trim, then add a belt around the cinched-in waist.

Now refine the hands, and start to create the swirling skirt of the greatcoat. Give the belt a big buckle.

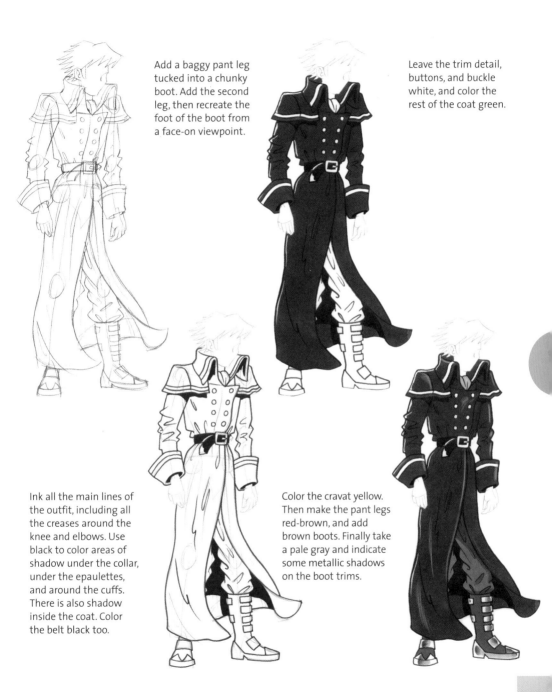

Add a baggy pant leg tucked into a chunky boot. Add the second leg, then recreate the foot of the boot from a face-on viewpoint.

Leave the trim detail, buttons, and buckle white, and color the rest of the coat green.

Ink all the main lines of the outfit, including all the creases around the knee and elbows. Use black to color areas of shadow under the collar, under the epaulettes, and around the cuffs. There is also shadow inside the coat. Color the belt black too.

Color the cravat yellow. Then make the pant legs red-brown, and add brown boots. Finally take a pale gray and indicate some metallic shadows on the boot trims.

LEATHER JACKET AND JEANS

This is a typical street biker look, with traditional leather jacket and scruffy pants. Note the lapel shape of the jacket, with studs and shoulder and wrist tabs. The pockets are diagonal slits with dangling fasteners, and there is a waistband. The character is also wearing fingerless leather gloves with vents on the back of the hand.

Draw a basic stick figure with lines for bones, circles for joints, and triangles for pelvis and feet. Add an open neck jacket to slightly below waist level.

Add double lapels with a button trim detail.

Now add loose baggy sleeves, and give the character gloved hands. Add the neck detailing of the teeshirt.

Draw pants, fitting at the waist, with some creases around the knees and baggy at the bottom. Then draw athletic shoes, and add a belt at the waist.

Ink the teeshirt, jacket, pants, gloves, and athletic shoes. Ink detail on the lapels, the chest, at the waist, and around the cuffs. Color the belt black; leave the buckle white.

THERMAL JUMPSUIT

Here is a futuristic-looking jumpsuit made of thermal all-weather material. The black bands indicate strapping and may be used for support or for attachments. The elbows are reinforced with heavyweight padding, and the soles are flat and functional. An outfit like this could be worn by itself or underneath a bulkier outfit such as a spacesuit or battlesuit.

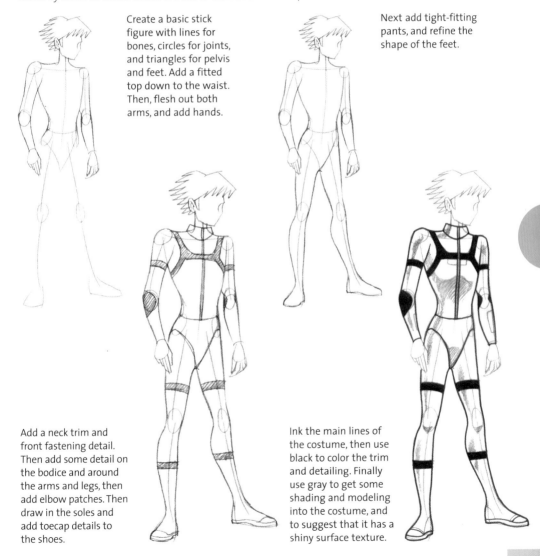

Create a basic stick figure with lines for bones, circles for joints, and triangles for pelvis and feet. Add a fitted top down to the waist. Then, flesh out both arms, and add hands.

Next add tight-fitting pants, and refine the shape of the feet.

Add a neck trim and front fastening detail. Then add some detail on the bodice and around the arms and legs, then add elbow patches. Then draw in the soles and add toecap details to the shoes.

Ink the main lines of the costume, then use black to color the trim and detailing. Finally use gray to get some shading and modeling into the costume, and to suggest that it has a shiny surface texture.

TECH BATTLE ARMOR

You can have a lot of fun with this kind of armor, adding attachments and items at random for a busy, technological feel. There is some visible weaponry on the right shoulder, with what looks like a cannon blaster of some sort. The antenna on the left shoulder suggests a communication device or transmitter, and the boots look rugged and heavy-duty.

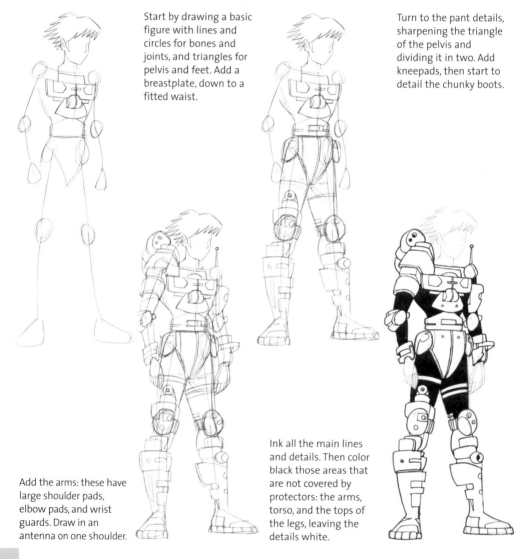

Start by drawing a basic figure with lines and circles for bones and joints, and triangles for pelvis and feet. Add a breastplate, down to a fitted waist.

Turn to the pant details, sharpening the triangle of the pelvis and dividing it in two. Add kneepads, then start to detail the chunky boots.

Add the arms: these have large shoulder pads, elbow pads, and wrist guards. Draw in an antenna on one shoulder.

Ink all the main lines and details. Then color black those areas that are not covered by protectors: the arms, torso, and the tops of the legs, leaving the details white.

Start to add shading to indicate a metallic finish to the protective shoulder, elbow and wrist pads, to the breastplate, to the pants, and to the boots.

Refine and sharpen the shading on the protective plates.

Finally, color the leg details bright yellow. A small splash of color on an otherwise dull-colored outfit like this can be very effective.

MONK ROBES

Priests and monks play a big part in many manga stories. This outfit consists of a plain brown under-robe, on top of which is worn a long flowing red robe, which is wrapped around the neck and shoulder before being tied at the waist, and hangs down to below the knee.

Create a basic figure using lines for bones, circles for joints, and triangles for pelvis and feet. Add a flowing sash over one shoulder and round the torso.

Draw the neckline with folds and creases, then add large flowing sleeves encasing the hands. Refine the waistline with a couple of horizontals.

From the waistline, create a full-length gathered double-skirt. Add a knotted sash at the waist. Finally at this stage, add flip-flops to the feet.

Ink all the main lines, trying to keep as many folds and creases in the drawing as you can: note there are creases around the elbows too. Then, color the inside of the sleeves black, as these areas are in shadow.

Color the left shoulder, sleeves, and under-robe using a flat dark brown.

Add color to the top robe using bright red, to give a nice contrast to the dull brown beneath.

Double up on color in the folds and creases to add greater realism. The folds on the top, around the waist, and on the skirt all need refining.

SWASHBUCKLING SWORDSMAN

Romantic tales of heroism and romance are very popular in manga. Here is an example of a typical dashing swordsman, with his graceful billowing blouse-top and tight-leg pants set off by a scarlet sash at the waist. His sword hangs at his side in a brown leather scabbard.

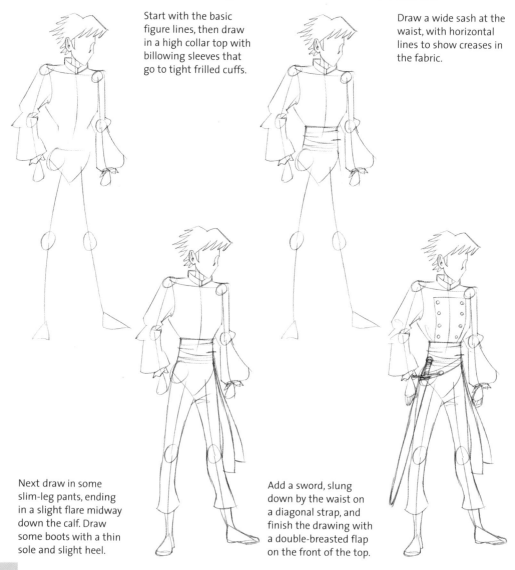

Start with the basic figure lines, then draw in a high collar top with billowing sleeves that go to tight frilled cuffs.

Draw a wide sash at the waist, with horizontal lines to show creases in the fabric.

Next draw in some slim-leg pants, ending in a slight flare midway down the calf. Draw some boots with a thin sole and slight heel.

Add a sword, slung down by the waist on a diagonal strap, and finish the drawing with a double-breasted flap on the front of the top.

Ink the main lines on your drawing, carefully indicating creases and folds on the top and at the groin.

Color the pants dark gray, and the sash bright red. Use a beige color to indicate shadows and folds on the white top, then color the scabbard brown, and the sword hilt gray-green.

Add some shadows to the pants with darker grays, and give the boots mauve shadows. Strengthen the beige shadows on the top with slightly darker shades.

177

SOLDIER

Occasionally manga tales may involve more realistic or contemporary military scenes. Army uniforms tend to follow a pattern such as that seen on this character. He's wearing a camouflaged battle uniform with helmet and utility belt, along with a backpack and sleeping roll. Below the knees he is wearing some strapping, known as puttees. These are a piece of cloth wrapped tightly round the calf from ankle to knee, and used as support.

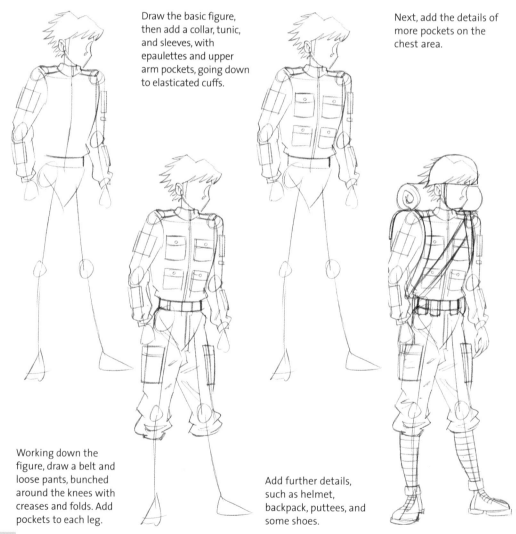

Draw the basic figure, then add a collar, tunic, and sleeves, with epaulettes and upper arm pockets, going down to elasticated cuffs.

Next, add the details of more pockets on the chest area.

Working down the figure, draw a belt and loose pants, bunched around the knees with creases and folds. Add pockets to each leg.

Add further details, such as helmet, backpack, puttees, and some shoes.

Now ink all the main lines and details of your drawing, using fineline pens as needed.

Color the basic uniform a yellow-green, and the puttees a dull ocher color, then color the boots brown.

Use a beige color on the bed roll and backpack, then add some dark-gray shading to the uniform in splotches.

Darken the center of the camouflage marks to give a more dynamic finish, and add some gray shading to the chest strap.

SPACESUIT

Here's a heavy-looking outfit designed to take the rigors of space travel, and possibly combat. The suit is extremely thick and has smooth curves to avoid radar detection. The surface of the suit is covered in a network of optical filaments and superconductors, which can help to disseminate friction when travelling at extreme speed.

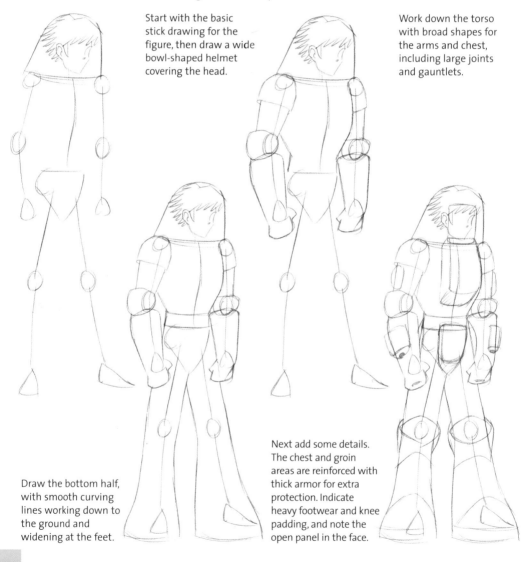

Start with the basic stick drawing for the figure, then draw a wide bowl-shaped helmet covering the head.

Work down the torso with broad shapes for the arms and chest, including large joints and gauntlets.

Draw the bottom half, with smooth curving lines working down to the ground and widening at the feet.

Next add some details. The chest and groin areas are reinforced with thick armor for extra protection. Indicate heavy footwear and knee padding, and note the open panel in the face.

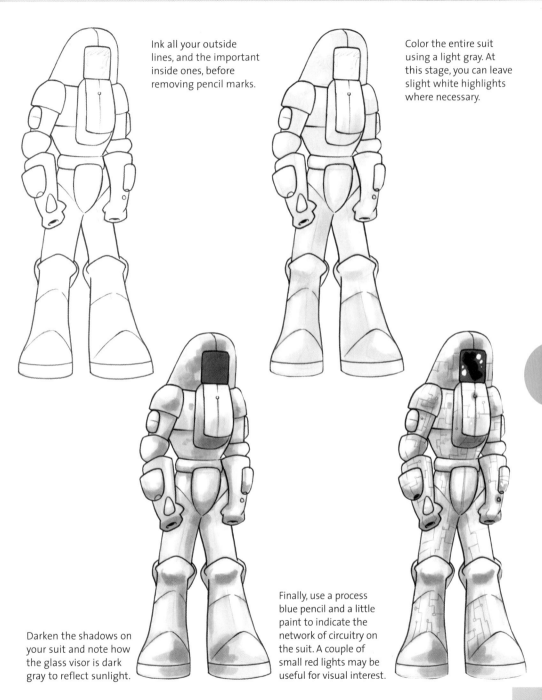

Ink all your outside lines, and the important inside ones, before removing pencil marks.

Color the entire suit using a light gray. At this stage, you can leave slight white highlights where necessary.

Darken the shadows on your suit and note how the glass visor is dark gray to reflect sunlight.

Finally, use a process blue pencil and a little paint to indicate the network of circuitry on the suit. A couple of small red lights may be useful for visual interest.

181

STREET FIGHTER

After military fighters, sword-fighters, and space-age fighters, it's back down to earth with a street fighter, who fights in secret bouts using similar skills but not knowing much about his opponent. The vest is torn at the sleeves, and he wears wristbands and a headband together with an arm strap for maximum effect.

Starting with the basic figure, add a curving waistline and a V-shaped neck.

Next add some baggy, loose pants with elasticated cuffs. Indicate some creases at the groin area.

Now draw fastenings on the front of the tunic, and add some sweatbands on his wrists. Sketch martial arts slippers.

Finish up with a headband and arm strapping, together with some neck pendants.

Ink your drawing carefully, using fine black pens.

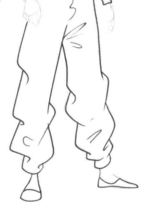

Color the tunic dark blue, and use pale blue-gray to put shadows on the white pants. The headband, wristbands, arm strap, and shoes should all be black.

Finally, darken and strengthen your shadows to give your drawing added impact.

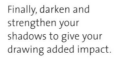

GALLERY

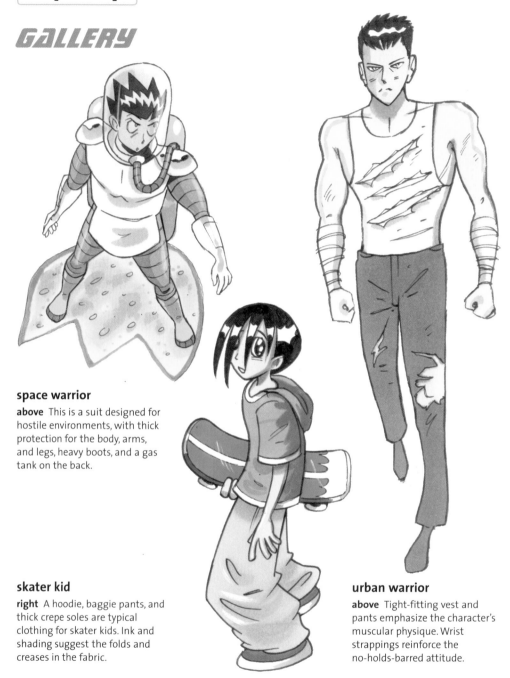

space warrior

above This is a suit designed for hostile environments, with thick protection for the body, arms, and legs, heavy boots, and a gas tank on the back.

skater kid

right A hoodie, baggie pants, and thick crepe soles are typical clothing for skater kids. Ink and shading suggest the folds and creases in the fabric.

urban warrior

above Tight-fitting vest and pants emphasize the character's muscular physique. Wrist strappings reinforce the no-holds-barred attitude.

martial arts

left Based on a martial arts uniform, this black suit is great for someone who has to move freely, as this character must do to dodge the shuriken stars.

eco fighter

below Pants and tunic, high boots, thick belt, and a warm cloak, all in earth colors, are suitable for an eco warrior.

young warrior

left A simple outfit of pants tucked into boots, tunic, and scarf is ideal for a young warrior. These clothes offer freedom of movement to wield the staff.

185

TOP AND SKIRT

This is a simple outfit that is easy to draw and suitable for a younger female character in a modern story. The top is fitted close to the body and the skirt is short and flares out from the hips. Socks and flat pumps are a common fashion item for girls in manga stories.

Create a figure from basic lines and ovals, and add face and hair. Flesh out the torso and arms, then create the profile of the breasts. Add a rounded neckline.

Finish the outline of the top at the waist and cuffs, then add a short skirt. Add flesh to the legs, and give the figure basic feet.

Outline the socks and Mary-Jane-style shoes. Give the socks typical ribbed cuffs.

Ink the outline of the top, skirt, and socks. Ink, too, creases at the elbows, under the breasts, and on the skirt. Use black ink to color the shoes.

Add some flat color. Here red has been used for the crop top, and gray for the skirt.

Finally, introduce some shading using darker tones of gray and red to suggest the folds in the fabric, and improve the modeling on the figure.

CITY SUIT

If your character works in an office, she might wear something like this smart two-piece suit, with a long sensible skirt and white blouse with a tie. Add a little splash of color with some caramel-colored loafers.

Draw a basic figure from lines and ovals, and add a face and hair. Start the outfit at the neck by drawing a collar, lapels, and a shaded necktie.

Complete the lines of the jacket, giving it a button trim, sleeves, and a breast pocket.

Next add a below-knee skirt, then flesh out the legs and feet, giving the character short socks, and athletic shoes.

Ink all the main lines. Color the tie black, then suggest creases at the elbows, under the breast, around the waist, and on the skirt. Outline the pocket trims.

Color the suit dark gray, and then make the shoes a pale shade of caramel. Leave white cuffs for the shirt, white buttons, and a white breast-pocket trim.

Finally work some subtle shading around the shoulders, along the arms, on the side, and in the shadow area created between the legs.

SUMMER HIKING

This is an outfit suitable for a summer hiking expedition, with a knitted sweater for keeping warm in the cool mountain air, and sensible shorts for warmer valleys. The colors are all earthy and natural, to emphasize the practical nature of the clothes. The sweater is a loose fit, as shown by the creases and folds around the waist and arms.

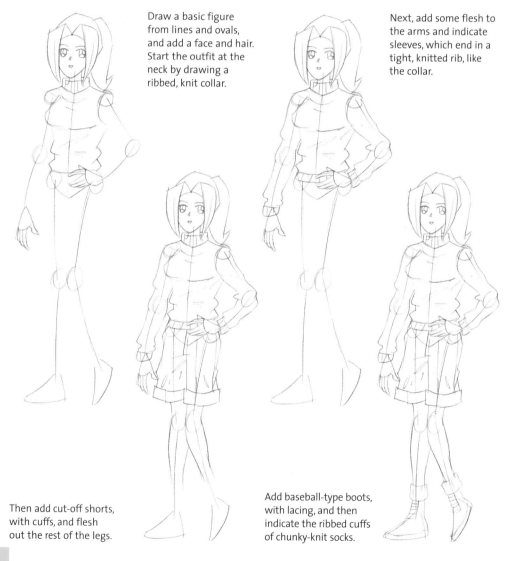

Draw a basic figure from lines and ovals, and add a face and hair. Start the outfit at the neck by drawing a ribbed, knit collar.

Next, add some flesh to the arms and indicate sleeves, which end in a tight, knitted rib, like the collar.

Then add cut-off shorts, with cuffs, and flesh out the rest of the legs.

Add baseball-type boots, with lacing, and then indicate the ribbed cuffs of chunky-knit socks.

Ink the main lines, and include an indication of folds and creases under the breasts and around the crotch area.

Add flat color: the top is brown and the shorts a shade of caramel. Then color the boots red-brown, leaving the laces white, and make the socks a shade of charcoal gray.

Finally add shading in darker tones, to give body and strength to your drawing.

SUMMER DRESS

Here's a simple but feminine summery dress, which has a bold stripy pattern and wide flowing skirt. This look suggests a happy, pleasant personality and an air of innocence, and would look appropriate for a country walk or a picnic in the park perhaps.

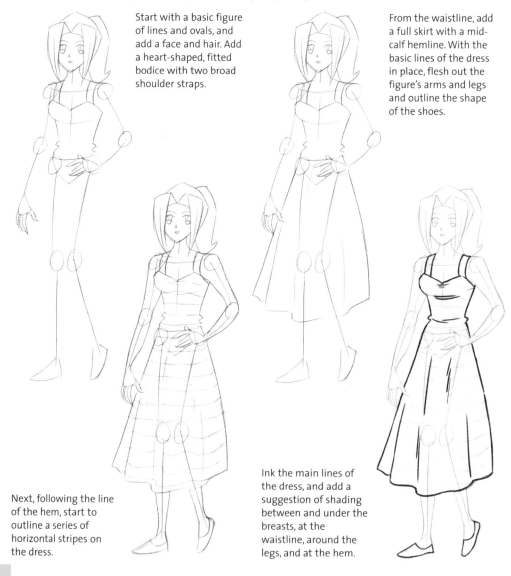

Start with a basic figure of lines and ovals, and add a face and hair. Add a heart-shaped, fitted bodice with two broad shoulder straps.

From the waistline, add a full skirt with a mid-calf hemline. With the basic lines of the dress in place, flesh out the figure's arms and legs and outline the shape of the shoes.

Next, following the line of the hem, start to outline a series of horizontal stripes on the dress.

Ink the main lines of the dress, and add a suggestion of shading between and under the breasts, at the waistline, around the legs, and at the hem.

Now outline in blue areas of horizontal stripes. Keep in mind the way fabric folds and drapes when you are drawing these lines.

Color between the lines you have drawn to create blue stripes. Also, color the shoulder straps blue. Then give her matching blue shoes.

Start to get some shading into the blue stripes, by adding more color into the folds in the fabric. Keep this consistent as you work down the dress.

Finish by echoing the darker areas of blue with cool gray shading on the white stripes of the dress.

SCHOOLGIRL

The school uniform is a very common form of dress in many manga stories. The outfit can vary from story to story, but is usually based on a simple sailor-style outfit like the one shown here. The collar is a broad V-shape, with a large bow tied underneath. The top itself is white, and is worn with a short pleated skirt.

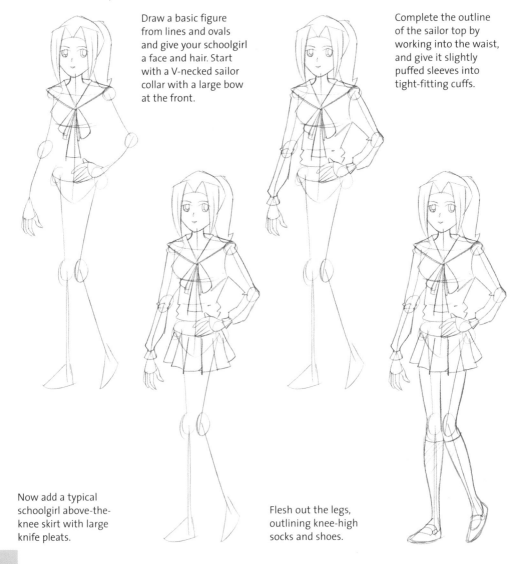

Draw a basic figure from lines and ovals and give your schoolgirl a face and hair. Start with a V-necked sailor collar with a large bow at the front.

Complete the outline of the sailor top by working into the waist, and give it slightly puffed sleeves into tight-fitting cuffs.

Now add a typical schoolgirl above-the-knee skirt with large knife pleats.

Flesh out the legs, outlining knee-high socks and shoes.

Ink the lines of the top, with its sailor collar, and of the pleated skirt. Ink, too, the tops and legs of the socks, and the main lines of the shoes.

Color the outfit. Typical colors are white with a blue collar for the shirt, and gray for the skirt. Make the socks black, and the shoes gray.

Finally, use a cool gray to sharpen the folds in the clothing, around the breast, under the collar, on the sleeves, and around the midriff.

POLLYANNA STYLE

Another popular style for manga females is the "Pollyanna," such as this example here. The look is frilly Victorian-era with a long flowing skirt and puffed sleeves. It can be used in a period story or as an eccentric alternative look in a modern-day tale.

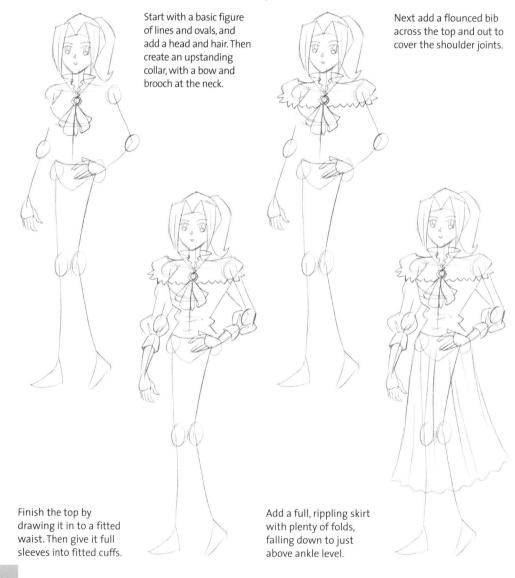

Start with a basic figure of lines and ovals, and add a head and hair. Then create an upstanding collar, with a bow and brooch at the neck.

Next add a flounced bib across the top and out to cover the shoulder joints.

Finish the top by drawing it in to a fitted waist. Then give it full sleeves into fitted cuffs.

Add a full, rippling skirt with plenty of folds, falling down to just above ankle level.

Add some underskirts or full petticoats for extra detail, then finish the look with high buttoned boots.

Color the main part of the dress a soft orange, using a deeper shade for the bow. Leave the flounces, collar, bib, and cuffs white. Go over your initial color to suggest folds and drapes in the fabric, under the bib, around the cuffs, at the waist, and in the skirt.

Use a fine pen to ink the main lines of the dress, including the bib, collar, and bow. Ink the individual flounces, then ink the shoes.

Finally color the neck bow a darker shade of orange. Add some gray shadow detail on the collar and work some darker orange shading into the dress under the breasts, on the sleeves, and on the skirt.

GIRL RACER

Here's a more streamlined look for a futuristic girl in a one-piece jumpsuit. The helmet could be for a high-powered motorbike, or part of a spacesuit. The suit is fitted closely around the neck with a zip fastener, and includes skintight gloves and boots. It has a bold, striking pattern in red and white, for high visibility.

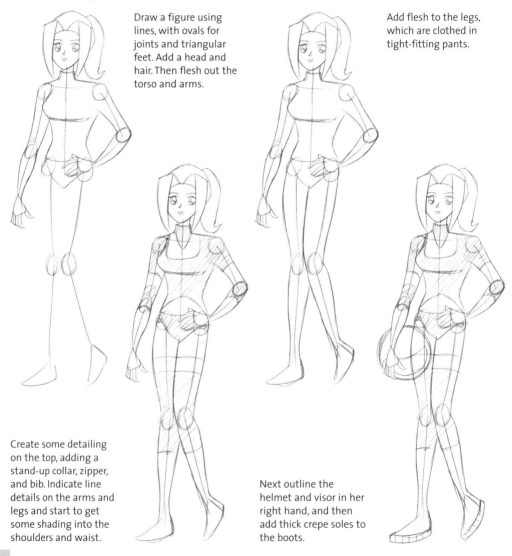

Draw a figure using lines, with ovals for joints and triangular feet. Add a head and hair. Then flesh out the torso and arms.

Add flesh to the legs, which are clothed in tight-fitting pants.

Create some detailing on the top, adding a stand-up collar, zipper, and bib. Indicate line details on the arms and legs and start to get some shading into the shoulders and waist.

Next outline the helmet and visor in her right hand, and then add thick crepe soles to the boots.

Ink the outline of the suit and the helmet, then ink over of the zipper and neck detail.

Color most of the top red, and add red detailing on the arms and around the legs. Make the boots red, and add red details on the helmet.

Finally add shading. Use a cool gray on the areas of white to get some modeling into them. Then double up the red at the shoulders, under the breast, and on the boots. Finally add white highlights on the shoulders, arms, and fronts of the legs.

197

WARRIOR WOMAN

Give your character a tough warrior look with this gladiator outfit, complete with leather-style sandals and slashed-open skirt flaps. The tunic is cut to the shoulders and buttoned across the lapels in a military style. Add arm coverings and wristbands, and complete the look with a headband.

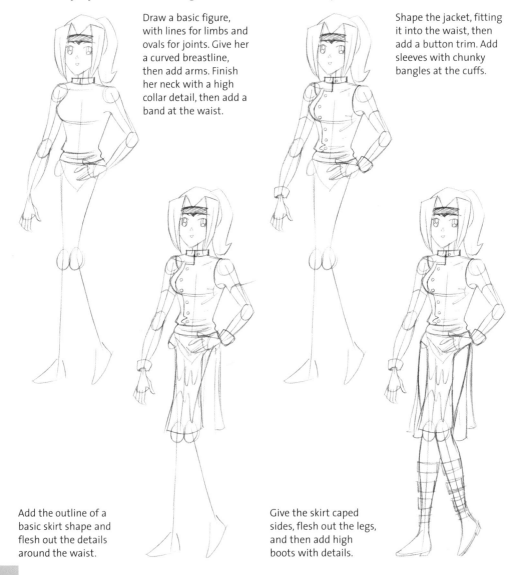

Draw a basic figure, with lines for limbs and ovals for joints. Give her a curved breastline, then add arms. Finish her neck with a high collar detail, then add a band at the waist.

Shape the jacket, fitting it into the waist, then add a button trim. Add sleeves with chunky bangles at the cuffs.

Add the outline of a basic skirt shape and flesh out the details around the waist.

Give the skirt caped sides, flesh out the legs, and then add high boots with details.

Ink the lines of the jacket, sleeves, bangles, skirt, and boots. Ink the buttons separately.

The color scheme here is yellow and green, so make the jacket and boots green, along with the bangles, while the skirt, sleeves, and boot trim are yellow. Leave some white highlights on the front of the jacket to suggest creases and folds.

Color the buttons yellow, then introduce some dark beige shading on the sleeves, in the folds of the skirt, and on the yellow trim on the boots.

TRENCH COAT

Lots of manga characters wear long flowing trench-coats like this one. The loose, flapping shape is great for dramatic effect and looks very elegant and stylish. Here the look is coupled with long thigh-length boots and heart-shaped top.

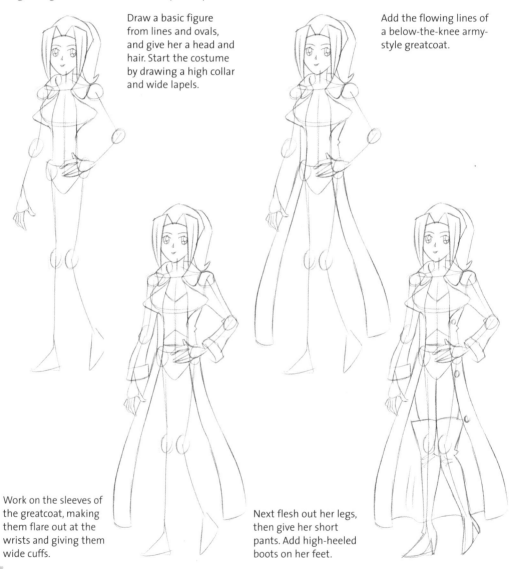

Draw a basic figure from lines and ovals, and give her a head and hair. Start the costume by drawing a high collar and wide lapels.

Add the flowing lines of a below-the-knee army-style greatcoat.

Work on the sleeves of the greatcoat, making them flare out at the wrists and giving them wide cuffs.

Next flesh out her legs, then give her short pants. Add high-heeled boots on her feet.

Ink the outline of the top, pants, coat, collar, lapels, and cuffs, and her legs. Then outline the buttons.

Color the pants chocolate brown and make the greatcoat honey, with a deeper brown lining.

Color the top a bright red, then add shadows to the coat with a dark gray-brown, and the boots with a cool gray. Finish with some white highlights on the sleeves and lapels.

EVENING DRESS WITH SCARF

For a sophisticated evening look suitable for all kinds of formal events and parties, try this long slimline evening dress and co-ordinating scarf. The cut is designed to follow the body in smooth curves, and is cut a little way up between the shins so that it flares out slightly. The scarf hangs casually over the shoulders and hangs down the back almost to the floor.

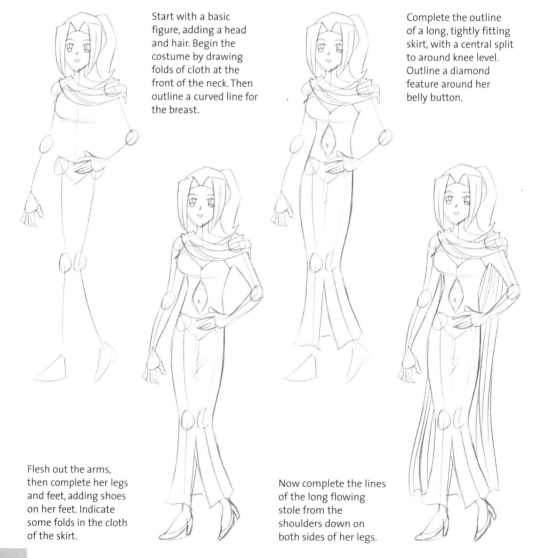

Start with a basic figure, adding a head and hair. Begin the costume by drawing folds of cloth at the front of the neck. Then outline a curved line for the breast.

Complete the outline of a long, tightly fitting skirt, with a central split to around knee level. Outline a diamond feature around her belly button.

Flesh out the arms, then complete her legs and feet, adding shoes on her feet. Indicate some folds in the cloth of the skirt.

Now complete the lines of the long flowing stole from the shoulders down on both sides of her legs.

Ink the lines of the dress and stole, and the shoes and ankle straps. Ink all the folds of the stole, then create some shading lines down the center of the dress and under the breasts.

Choose a strong acid green for the dress, leaving the area around her navel white. Then use a dark green for the long, draped stole. Color her shoes dark gray.

Take darker shades of both greens to create the shadows of folds and creases in the clothes. Outline the line of her legs, to highlight the sleek profile of the dress.

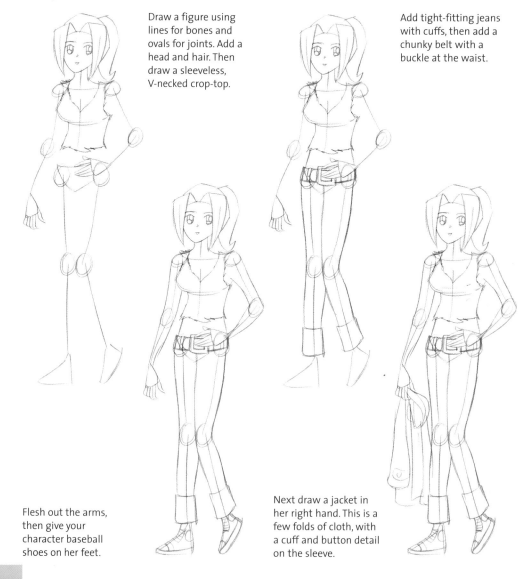

CROP-TOP AND JEANS

This is a casual street look for a cool young female. The style is slightly punk, with a torn, sleeveless teeshirt, jeans with high turn-ups, and red baseball shoes, and she's holding a jacket loosely in her hand.

Draw a figure using lines for bones and ovals for joints. Add a head and hair. Then draw a sleeveless, V-necked crop-top.

Add tight-fitting jeans with cuffs, then add a chunky belt with a buckle at the waist.

Flesh out the arms, then give your character baseball shoes on her feet.

Next draw a jacket in her right hand. This is a few folds of cloth, with a cuff and button detail on the sleeve.

Ink your sketch. Make the crop-top edges read as torn. Ink in the fly and all the belt and buckle details. Then ink the profile of the breast and some creases around the crotch.

Color the jeans blue, with pale blue cuffs. Make the belt black, leaving the buckle white, then give her bright red shoes.

Work the jacket in shades of gray, then use a light gray on the top to get some shading here. Finally add shadows to the jeans using darker shades of blue.

BATTLE ARMOR

If your character is facing battle in the far reaches of space, a suit of reinforced metallic armor like this is essential. The armor itself covers the most vulnerable areas of the body, and is worn over a thin flexible black leotard made of extra-strength thread. Armor can be drawn as a series of randomly assorted shapes, but must be convincing to the viewer.

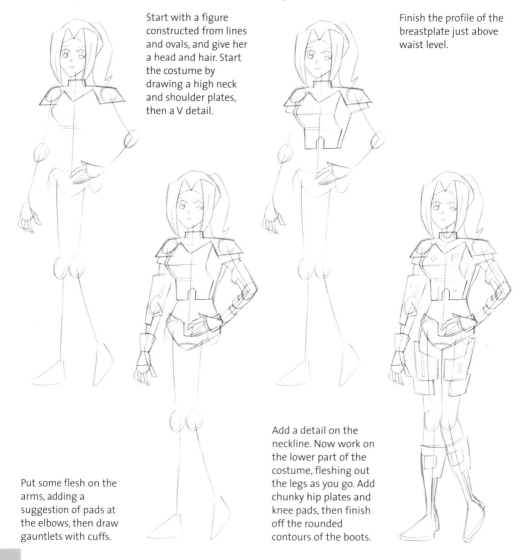

Start with a figure constructed from lines and ovals, and give her a head and hair. Start the costume by drawing a high neck and shoulder plates, then a V detail.

Finish the profile of the breastplate just above waist level.

Put some flesh on the arms, adding a suggestion of pads at the elbows, then draw gauntlets with cuffs.

Add a detail on the neckline. Now work on the lower part of the costume, fleshing out the legs as you go. Add chunky hip plates and knee pads, then finish off the rounded contours of the boots.

Ink all the main lines to define the shape of the costume more closely: the shoulders and breastplate are fairly square, as are the hip guards and knee plates.

Color the leotard black to make the metallic armor pieces stand out.

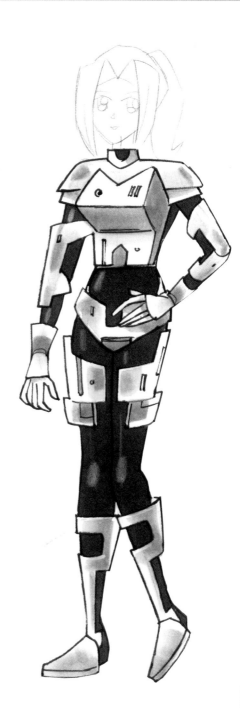

Use a variety of grays to add shading to the armor pieces, suggesting a metallic finish, and make the shadows darker where necessary. Add a little white highlighting on the knees and hips for extra depth.

GALLERY

period style

below Stories with period settings are popular in several manga subgenres, and it can be great fun drawing historical fashions on your characters.

chibi

above There are stories for all age groups in manga. For the very young, the "chibi" style, in which normal characters are compressed into exaggerated, cute proportions, such as this figure, is very popular.

fashionable

right This is a contemporary figure. Japanese girls can be very fashion-conscious and this is reflected in some modern manga stories.

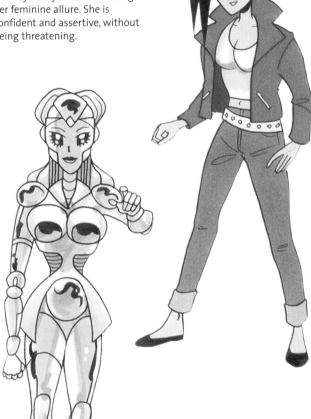

tomboy

right Manga girls can be fashionable as well as cute, and this girl shows a tough, tomboyish style without losing her feminine allure. She is confident and assertive, without being threatening.

schoolgirl

above The sailor-suit school uniform is a common sight in manga, as are stories with a school theme.

other-worldly

left Manga females and their costumes are not always human, although this robotic figure has definite female characteristics.

209

Accessories

You can have a lot of fun with accessories and gadgets, and it is worth practicing drawing them. A simple touch such as a helmet or belt can really make a character stand out, and give him or her (or it!) a unique identity. Use the examples here as just a starting point: there is no limit to your imagination in devising accessories.

BASEBALL CAP

The baseball cap is one of the most common forms of headgear, and is easy to draw. Hats can be a useful accessory to individualize a character. This one is a standard shape, with a curving peak and a vent at the back. The panels of the cap alternate betwen yellow and white, and there is a white button on top.

Start with a basic head shape, and establish an eye line.

Sketch in positions for the eyes, nose, and mouth, then draw a line circling the head just above the eyeline.

Then establish the lines of the cap's peak: these consist of two curves and two horizontals. Add in the vent detail, and the button on the crown.

 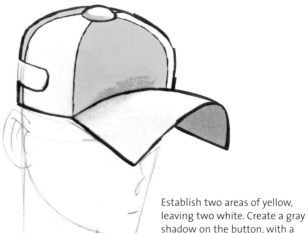

Ink the lines you established in pencil using a medium nib, then with a thinner nib outline stitching lines on the crown.

Establish two areas of yellow, leaving two white. Create a gray shadow on the button, with a deeper gray under the peak.

HEADPHONES

Headgear isn't just about hats. This character wears large, old-fashioned headphones with cushioned earpieces. He could be a music-loving teen, a helicopter pilot, or somebody on surveillance duty at a stake-out.

Create a basic oval head, adding a curving line on the right to get the eyeline on that side of the face. This helps you to get the lines of the pad later.

Add basic features of eyes and brows, nose, and mouth. Then create the ovals of the pads on both sides of the head.

The phones and pads are constructed from circles and ovals in perspective. Add the lines of the headpiece, and a curl flex. Finally sketch in some hair.

Ink the main lines you have established, varying the thickness of the nib for the different areas of the phones and pads.

Leaving white highlights, color the pads gray. Use brown for the headpiece, phones, and flex, with red for the detailing.

TECH SPECS

Eyewear is another good accessory for your manga characters. These are serious-looking glasses with a tinted visor, and a heavy, metallic frame that looks like it could contain some electronic hardware. Note how the tint on the lens is a gradient, which gives it extra realism.

Draw a basic head shape using a circle and curving lines down to the chin, and indicate two vertical lines for the neck.

Sketch in the eyes, ears, nose and mouth, then draw a curving horizontal band across the top of the eye level.

From here, add the lines of the lenses, which are essentially half circles. Create the large joints for the earpieces, then give the character some spiky hair.

Ink the lines of the eyes, and then all the main lines of the frame, earpieces, and lenses.

Leaving white highlights to suggest reflections, color the lenses brown. Then use a mauve gray for details on the crosspieces and earpiece, with ice blue above the nose.

SPY GOGGLES

Goggles are another form of eyewear. They could be night-vision or infra-red. The straps sit across the top of the head to give a firm fit, and the dials on either side of the goggles may be used for focus or mode switching. The lenses are large, camera-like pieces for a powerful look.

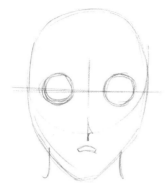

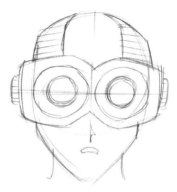

Start with a circular shape for the head, then draw two curving lines down to a pointed chin. Add two short verticals for the neck.

Draw a horizontal for the eye and ear line, with a vertical center line. Position the nose and mouth, then draw two circles for the goggles' lenses.

Add more detail of the frames with two larger circles, then create the shape of the frame. Add earpieces, then work some details into the head.

Ink all the lines, using two thicknesses of nib. Then using black ink to color the lenses, leaving three white highlights in each.

Introduce color into the headpieces and around the lenses, frame, and earpieces. Then use gray for shadow areas around the lenses and under the eyepieces.

HEADBAND

This scarlet sash tied around the head can give your character a touch of drama and bravery. It can be a good accessory for a warrior or street fighter, or just someone with a devil-may-care attitude to life. Note how the shading with horizontal lines gives the fabric a realistic look.

Draw a circle for the head, with two curving lines down to a pointed chin. Add a horizontal for the neck.

Now add horizontals to help position the eyes and eyebrows, and two more for the top and bottom of the headband. Add a nose and a mouth.

Create the ear, using the eyeline as a guide to position. Then give the character thick spikes of hair on top of the head. Finally, create the rounded lines of the headband.

Ink the folds and creases of the headband, creating some thick lines to give it some texture.

Finally color the headband bright red.

NINJA-STYLE HEADWRAP

A more austere look is this all-over head-and-neck wrap, in the style of a ninja warrior. Ninjas usually favor dark colours such as black, dark blue, and dark red, but can also wear white and other colors. Usually the lower half of the face is also covered, but here the look is open-faced. Note the white highlights across the forehead which give a full, rounded look.

Start with a circle, then draw two lines down to a pointed chin. Create the profile of the chin, then add lines for the neck.

Add a horizontal eyeline, then position eyes, eyebrows, nose, and mouth. Refine the jawline, then add the horizontal for the bottom of the headpiece.

Create the profile of the headpiece by sharpening the line of the crown, and creating two verticals for the sidepiece. Then add its line under the chin.

Use a medium-nibbed pen to ink the main lines of the profile of the headpiece, and then add some ink lines to suggest folds and creases in the fabric.

Leave some areas of white highlight on top of the head to help with modeling, then color the headpiece dark blue. Add darker color down the sides and under the chin.

FINGERLESS FIGHTING GLOVES

These studded leather gloves are good for a tough, streetwise character who may be a gang member or otherwise involved in violent activities. The knuckles are studded with short metallic spikes and the fingers are left open for extra flexibility.

Draw a hand from basic shapes, with four simple rounded rectangles for fingers.

Create the shape of the fingerless glove. Draw the line of the cuff with a stud detail. Add circles for the knuckles and for the glove details.

Ink over all the lines to outline the shape of the glove. Ink the knuckle detail, then suggest some creasing around the wristline and the bottom of the fingers.

Color the glove purple-gray, then add darker grays for shadows and texture. Use a pale blue to add a hint of steel to the studs on the knuckle line.

EXOTIC RINGS

This colorful collection of rings could be ideal for a fantasy story with a wizard or sorcerer of some kind. Each ring looks magical in its own way, and the ring on the little finger has a skull-like motif to convey an air of danger. The brightly colored centerpieces on the other rings have multiple white highlights to show reflections.

Draw a basic fist using right angles for the fingers. Add the joints of the closest finger, and outline the thumb.

Add a fantasy ring to each finger, diminishing in size from the first finger down to the little finger.

Ink the major lines of the rings, outlining all the details you worked up in pencil.

Color your rings using a variety of colors. Leave white highlights. Finally, work up some gray shadows to suggest that the rings are metallic.

GALLERY

bracelet

below This bracelet has a decorative, traditional look, but it could also be turned into a futuristic weapon.

cute pet

above If all else fails, nothing works better than a sidekick. A colorful pet such as this provides a confidant for the character, and offers plenty of opportunities for laughs.

gauntlet

below This looks like a weapon. The dull gray color gives a no-nonsense, functional look.

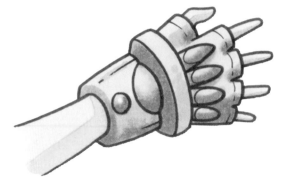

necklace

above This necklace could grace a tribal queen in official dress. The gold gives an air of wealth, but the curved spikes look like teeth from a jungle beast.

winged hat

below The owner of this baseball cap with its quirky twist could be a fun-loving teen.

belt

above This belt has a colorful, military-style buckle, and could be part of a uniform.

strap

right A big leather strap and buckle is great for a swashbuckler or a pirate.

earrings

right Earrings such as this one have a rebellious, non-conformist feel, especially when they are added to a pointy ear.

goggles

above These look like they are serious night-vision hardware. Goggles can add a great deal to any street character.

WRISTBAND

Here is a weighty-looking wristband or bracelet. The extra-thick shape has a series of what appear to be carved grooves, which give a suggestion of technology, but the texture and color look almost stone-like and primitive. It could be an alien artifact, or a relic discovered on an archeological dig. The fist implies it is a weapon of some kind though.

Start with a basic fist, created from angled lines. Add a sausage-shaped thumb across the fingers.

Now create the outline of a chunky wristband from circular lines. Make one tight around the wrist, and two more to give it a profile. Add chevron patterns and some circle details.

Ink the wristband, including the details. Then ink around the wrist to establish the inner profile of the wristband.

Color the wristband yellow, then work up the details in a more golden shade. Create brown shadows under the wristband.

CLAWS

Give your manga character a feral, animal look with these dangerous-looking claws. They extend in long curves out from each fingernail, and are colored shiny black for extra menace. The fingers here are slender and feminine, which suggests a cat-like attitude.

Start with a basic open hand with four fingers and a thumb.

Now draw superlong pointed fingernails from all the fingers and the thumb, starting from the rounded cuticles.

Outline the areas of fingernail using black ink.

Leaving areas of white highlight on each nail, color them shiny black.

POWER GAUNTLET

This is a heavyweight piece of hardware, with a hefty metallic gauntlet studded with what could be lasers or projectile-launchers. The fingertips are open to enable a more delicate control, and the back of the hand appears to have a main firing button.

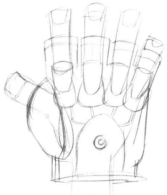

Draw a hand using basic shapes. making the back, wrist, fingers, and thumb.

Now create the outline of the gauntlet. Take the fingers up to the first joints, work some detailing around the base of the fingers, and add a shield shape to the back of the hand.

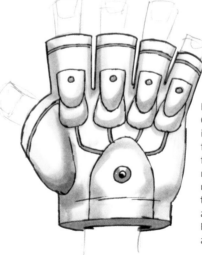

Ink over all the detailed lines you worked in pencil, including the fine lines at the ends of the fingers of the glove. Then ink the shields on the joints and back of the hand, and the jewel.

Keep the color minimal. Color the jewel setting ice blue , and use blue for the line details and finger studs. Then use mauve to get some rounded modeling into the hand and fingers, and onto the thumb. Finally add gray shading around the wrist.

GOLDEN BANGLE

This finely crafted bangle is made from pure gold, and would be a fitting decoration for a manga princess or royalty of some kind, as suggested by the slender, feminine hand and wrist. The shape is simple and elegant, with a cut-away ellipse on the back, and large gold studs circling the wrist.

Create a basic hand with a long, slender wrist, back of the hand, and four fingers.

Now draw a fine, broad bracelet around the wrist. Give it a U-shaped detail, then add two full studs and the profiles of two more for its decoration.

Ink the outline of the bracelet, its U-detail profile, and studs. Then ink darker areas on both sides to suggest modeling. Create shadow around the wrist.

Use honey gold to strengthen the effect of a metal bracelet. Leave areas white on the bracelet and the studs, to suggest their rounded shapes.

DEMON TAIL

An appendage like this demonic-looking tail can be a great way to give your character a memorable and unusual accessory. It has a slightly devilish look, but does not necessarily imply an evil personality and can just as readily be used on a cute, monkey-like figure.

Create a body from basic shapes, fleshing out the arms and legs so that you have the running profile of a figure.

Draw a curling S-shape up and out from the buttocks. Flesh this out with a line either side, then give it a pointed end.

Start inking from above the buttocks, taking the line up the tail, around the point, and back into the buttock. Start a new line to create the top of the leg.

Use two shades of reptilian greens, with some white modeling to make the shape of the tail.

TRIBAL AMULET

If your character is in a primitive tribal setting, or perhaps in a rural historical scenario, she may be wearing something like this amulet. There are a pair of chunky-looking gemstones, fixed by leather straps into a neck ornament.

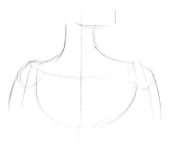

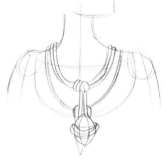

Use basic shapes to create the outline of shoulders, neck, and upper chest. Flesh out the upper arms, and add a breastline.

Start with a string of three curving lines, then add two deeper curved lines. Hang a thin triangle from the bottom string, add an oval detail, then create a knotted detail to join the two.

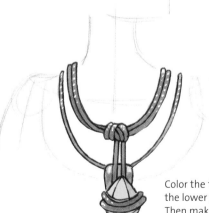

Ink the lines in the order you drew them: the knot on the upper string should read in front of the triangle, and the strings on the lower sit on top of it.

Color the triangle pale green and the lower jewel in shades of gold. Then make all the strings leather-colored. Finally, add some tiny white highlights to the leather thongs.

CAT EARS

A peculiar feature of manga stories is the way some characters sport random animal characteristics, such as these cat-like ears. Sometimes these features are used to denote a certain quirky personality trait, and sometimes to signify an alien race or fantasy humanoid. The ears can be worn in tandem with a tail for extra effect, but the figure would be otherwise human.

Draw an oval, then refine its profile. Add a horizontal for the eyeline, then draw large, innocent eyes. Add a tiny nose and mouth.

Starting from the line at the top of the head, outline two triangular ears, with inner ears. Then create a short, spiky fringe, and body of hair.

Ink the two sets of lines for both ears, and then ink the line at the base on the ear on the right.

Color the outer ears brown and the inner ear pale pink.

FANTASY HELMET

Here's another character with animalistic ears, this time with the added accessory of a fantastical-looking helmet. The ears resemble a kid goat, and the hat is reminiscent of a toadstool, so the overall effect is cute and whimsical, and would suit a fantasy tale of woodland folk perhaps.

Start with an oval for the head. Add a curved horizontal and position large eyes with highlights on it. Add a tiny nose, mouth, and ear.

Work a double line out from the center of the head on both sides to create the brim. Add a domed profile, with central trim. Add button details down this trim.

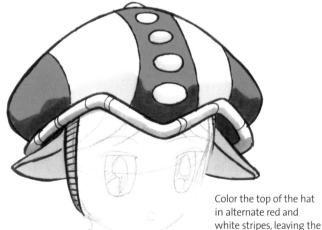

Ink all the main lines of the profile and trim, the main band, and the ears.

Color the top of the hat in alternate red and white stripes, leaving the button trim white. Make the ears pale green, then get some gray shading into the brim.

SHOULDER BAG

An everyday accessory could be this practical-looking shoulder bag, with a flap-over cover and buckle fastening, and a zip-fastened pocket on the front. Bags like this are very common, but an individual bag can come to be associated with a particular character. Note the way it hangs across from one shoulder to the opposite hip.

Draw a torso using basic shapes for joints and lines for bones, then flesh out the torso and arms. Outline a teeshirt and add a belt at the waist.

Add a double line for a shoulder strap over the shoulder and under the arm. Create a front and welt for the bag, adding trim details and buckles.

Ink the lines of the bag, outlining all the details of the belts and buckles, the pockets and name-badge holder. Ink some shading on the strap.

Leaving the buckles and trims white, and areas of white on the top of the bag to help with its overall shape, color the bag bright blue.

CRASH HELMET

Perhaps your character is a star racing driver, or a space pilot. If so, they may need some smart headgear like this blue and yellow crash helmet. Helmets are usually a smooth, circular shape, and can have a cut-away face like this one, or be fully enclosed with just the eyes visible. The visor should fall down to the nose level, and may be tinted to reduce glare and reflection.

Start with an oval, then draw two lines down from it to a pointed chin. Add a neck, then create an eyeline. Refine the profile on the right, then draw in eyes with highlights, eyebrows, nose, and mouth.

Draw a large, circular shape to create the outline of a helmet. Add a horizontal across the forehead and bring this down on both sides to chin level, then round off. Finally, add the line of the base of the visor across the nose and out to both sides.

Use a medium nib to ink the outline of the helmet and visor. Then with a thinner pen, ink in stripe details and outline two stars. Finally, ink the eyes, eyebrows, and top of the nose.

Color the top of the helmet bright blue, with a pale blue side. Work the color around the stars. Color the stripe details gold. Make the eyes blue. Then shade the visor blue-gray.

ELBOW AND WRIST GUARDS

A teenage character might be speeding around on a skateboard, or inline skates, and if so he or she may need to wear protective accessories like these elbow guards and wrist supports. Notice how the elbow guard cups the elbow for maximum protection and comfort.

Use circles for shoulder and elbow joints with lines for bones, then flesh out arms, with a thin wrist and hand with four fingers and a thumb. Flesh out a basic torso and the top of a leg.

Refine the profile of a top, then work in a rounded protector over the elbow joint. Add the strap at the crook of the elbow. Next add a double band at the wrist.

Color the elbow pad purple, then use gray to get some shading into the white areas. Color the strap and the wrist band brown, leaving a white highlight with gray shading.

Outline the elbow pad, then work the pattern on it. Add some stripes on the strap. Then ink the detail on the wrist guard.

KNEEPADS

These kneepads are an ideal accessory to go with the elbow guards. They are molded to fit the knee and protect against any crash landings your character may have to suffer. The striped grooves are designed to reduce the stress on the overall shape, as well as being a decorative touch. And they're fastened behind the knee with adjustable strapping.

Draw ovals for knee joints and lines for bones, then flesh out the profiles of two legs. Add boots to both legs.

Now create the knee pads, which are essentially triangles, with zigzag details. Indicate the strap at the back.

Ink the lines of the pads, taking care that they read as two separate pads, one for each knee with the front one slightly obscuring the back.

Working around the detailing at the top, color the main parts of the pads dark green, then use brown for the zigzag detail and the strap. Add some shading to the white details.

233

NERD GLASSES

Nerdy, intelligent characters are a familiar sight in manga stories, and these classic spectacles are an ideal way to suggest this type of personality. The shape of the lenses should be large and round, with simple thin wire frames that curl right round behind the ears. You can add a slight gradient tint and some white highlights to suggest reflection.

Draw a circle for the head, with lines down to a pointed chin. Add an eyeline and draw eyes and an ear to this line. Add a nose and mouth, and some spiky hair.

Create large round spectacles by drawing a couple of circles, then joining them with a bridge. Finally add an earpiece.

Outline the main lines of the spectacles in ink, then ink in the outlines of the iris.

Use a pale cool blue to get some color into the lenses, suggesting that they are made of glass.

CROSSED BELTS

A more swashbuckling look is this crossed-belt arrangement, slung down on either side of the hips. The belts can be contrasting colors. They have large buckles, and would be suitable for a cool, fashionable character or even a gunslinger. Note how the eyeholes are evenly spaced along the length of the belt.

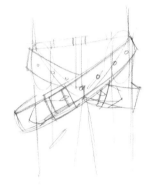

Create a basic torso from above the waist to above the knee. Draw a belt and fly. Then criss-cross the pants with lines to suggest creases.

Draw in a crossed belt, fitting at the waist and looser lower down. Indicate the buckle holes, with one whole buckle and one partially obscured one.

Define the outline of the belt, creating a three-dimensional profile at the top of both parts of the belt. Ink all the details.

Leaving the buckles white, color the belt using browns to indicate leather. Finally get some shading into the buckles using gray for a metallic look.

SCARF

In a blizzard, dust storm, or gas cloud, a face-covering scarf like this can be a useful accessory. It covers the nose and mouth, and folds around the neck where it's tied. Behind you can see the remainder of the scarf trailing in the breeze in two rippling strands, which gives a good dramatic visual effect.

Create a basic head, with a pointed chin and a suggestion of spiky hair. Add an eyeline and position eyes and ears. Square off the jaw and the top of the head.

Now start to cover the bottom of the nose, the mouth, and the neck area, and the top of the chest with a series of loose flowing lines of fabric.

Next add the two tails of the fabric, trailing out behind the figure to suggest movement.

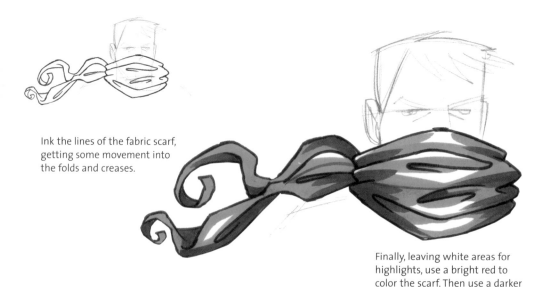

Ink the lines of the fabric scarf, getting some movement into the folds and creases.

Finally, leaving white areas for highlights, use a bright red to color the scarf. Then use a darker red to get some shading into the folds in the fabric.

EYEPATCH

This eyepatch and scar combination is a great way to give a character a menacing, thuggish aspect. The patch is held on by an elastic strap which runs diagonally across the head and behind the ear. The scar runs in a curve down from the nostril toward the lower jaw, and looks like it came in a fight. Note the shape of this character's head and features, which all add to the look. The shading on the eyepatch is slightly graduated to give the impression of a curved surface.

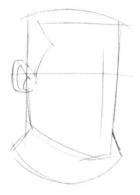

Use basic shapes to create a fairly square head with a pointed chin and simple hair profile. Add an eyeline and draw in an ear. Add a vertical center line.

Draw one eye and eyebrow on the eyeline. Add an eyepatch where the second eye would be positioned, taking the strap out to the ear and up over the other eye. Add a nose and mouth.

To add to the character's mystery air, draw in a livid scar with lines for the scars of stitches.

Ink the outline of the patch, the straps of the patch, and the lines of the scar.

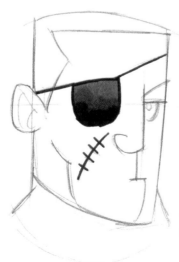

Then color the eyepatch very dark gray.

EARRING

Another type of jewelry you can dress your character with are earrings. These can be simple or more elaborate like these ornate examples. The stud is supporting a string of small beads, followed by a gem in a clasp, and some hook-shaped attachments in alternative colors.

Create the profile of an ear, paying attention to the whorls inside, and the basic shape of the lobe where the earring will sit.

Draw a circle on the earlobe, then a series of smaller circles for the jewels hanging down. Then add a large jewel.

To finish the drawing, add a few chunky U-shaped jewels.

Ink over all the lines of the earring, outlining the details.

Use ice blue to color some of the jewels, together with pale lime green. As you color, leave white highlights to suggest the shimmer on the jewels.

WRIST STRAPPINGS

Your manga character may be a street fighter, in which case he may wear these wrist wraps as a support accessory. They focus the viewer's attention on the hands, and emphasize the no-holds-barred attitude to combat that a street-fighter has, which can instill a nervous apprehension in an opponent and aid a fighter's victory.

Create a hand from basic shapes: circles for joints and lines for bones. Flesh out the hand. Add a long, thin wrist.

Add some pairs of lines from the knuckles to the top of the wrist. Keep the pairs randomly spaced but parallel to each other.

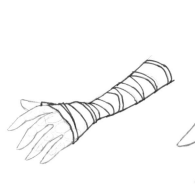

Ink over the lines, including the profile of the arm.

Color the wrist using mauve, and leave some areas white to get some rounded modeling into the shape of the arm.

GALLERY

hair ribbon

right A simple, pretty ribbon can add cuteness to any girl character, and add color and visual interest to her hair.

boot

above Sturdy, all-purpose boots are a must in all kinds of situations. They can be sturdy like this one, or more dainty for a cuter, more feminine look.

bracelet

above Any girl can be given added glamour by adding some sparkling bangles and bracelets like these.

wings

below Fantasy is an important part of manga, so you could give your character a lift with a beautiful pair of wings.

knife sheath

above This knife strapped onto her leg of an adventurous action girl, could prove vital in a steamy jungle setting.

goggles

right Anti-glare goggles like these could be useful in a polar landscape or a sun-drenched desert world.

headband

above Another interesting head accessory is this classic-looking headband. Use it for a royal princess or as part of a magical girl's armory.

necklace/amulet

above Jewelry adds a touch of glamour, and can also be a magical talisman for any girl.

vanity bag

above Feminine and functional, a bag like this could be used to carry vital ingredients for a magic spell. It needs to be carefully color-coordinated.

glove

left A thick, chunky glove is an ideal accessory for a fighter or a street character.

Animals

Animals in manga can be cute and cuddly or large and fearsome. They are ideal pets and confidants, or enemies to be battled in the woods and on the streets. Most manga animals are derived from recognizable creatures, but taken at least one stage further through coloring or additional fantasy features.

CUDDLY BEAR

Here's a friendly-looking bear in a cute manga style, walking up on his hind legs. His face has a serene, gentle expression, and his markings are in simplified tones of chocolate brown and beige. Little details such as the claws on his feet and hands give a nice finishing touch to the drawing.

Start with basic shapes, drawing an oval for the body, with a circle for a head on top.

Add a couple of semicircles for ears, then add two arm shapes. Create two bear-like legs.

Flesh out a cute, teddy bear face. Add eyes with pupils and double highlights, nose, and smiling mouth. Add a pad to its left paw and three claws. Then add claws to the feet.

Ink all the main lines, and use black to color the pupils, working around the highlights.

Color your animal brown, with a honey-colored face, tummy, inner ears, and pad. Work the underside of the snout in black.

BEAR ON ALL FOURS

Here's our cuddly bear again, but this time he's walking on all fours in a more natural bear-like posture. You can see how the head sits down low in relation to the big elliptical body, and how the four paws are at each corner to balance the weight.

Start with a circle for the head, then draw an oval behind it for the body.

Add two semicircles to the top of the head for ears. Then draw in the legs, one at each "corner" of your bear.

Create the face, adding a facemask, eyes, snout, and mouth. Draw the inner ear, then draw claws on all four feet.

Ink around the main lines of your sketch. Color the pupils black, then ink some shading detail on the legs and forehead.

Color your bear brown, with a honey-colored face and underbelly. Color the lower part of his snout black. Finally create some modeling using white.

HERO DOG IN PROFILE

Dogs are very popular pets in Japan, and feature in many manga stories. This dog is a generic snow-white hound with an appealing expression and a heroic aspect. His straight back, healthy coat, and alert eyes all add to the impression of a loyal and devoted companion.

Draw basic shapes to start with: circles for the head, rump, knee joints, and feet. Use lines for the leg bones, and join the head and rump with a basic oval.

Flesh out the body, giving the back a curved profile. Add flesh to the legs, and create a bushy tail. Then add a couple of rectangles to the face.

Create the profile of the face, adding ears and an eye, a snout, and a tongue. Add a collar, then indicate the lines of the toes on the paws.

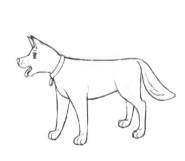 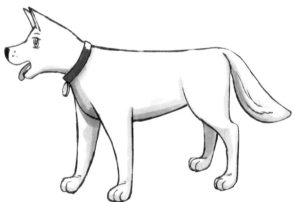

Get some modeling into the animal by using subtle shading on the belly, under the tail, and on the legs. Color the tongue pink, and make the collar dark gray.

Ink your sketch, making the eye black, and adding a couple of lines to the tail.

BARKING DOG

This dog is adopting a classic "Stay back! This is my territory!" pose. His forelegs are set wide to present the largest possible front, and the hindlegs are poised for leaping forward if necessary. The mouth is wide open in a furious bark, fangs bared and the eyes have a fierce stare. The jagged black lines above the head represent noise and tension.

Draw circles for the head and rump, and circles for the leg joints and feet. Join these with lines for the bones of the leg.

Add flesh to the legs and paws, and create the profile of the breastbone between the front legs. Add the swinging tail.

Get some detail into the face, adding ears, eyes, snout, and large open mouth. Draw fangs and the tongue, then add a collar and tag.

Now ink all the main lines of your dog. Add shadow lines around the eyes, and ink the individual joints on the feet.

Use subtle gray shading to get some modeling into the dog. Use pale pink for his tongue, with darker pink inside the mouth. Finally, add emphatic black lines to indicate barking.

SITTING KITTY

Cats are much more serene than dogs. This cat is sitting in a typical cat pose, with tail swishing out behind. The expression is content, but with a slightly mischievous air, as shown by the arched eye shape and curled-up smile. The eyes are drawn in a manga style, with large black pupils and twin highlights.

Start by drawing a circle for the head, then an oval for the basic body shape. Use curved lines for the shape of the front legs, with two circles for the paws.

Now add flesh to the two front legs, then create the profile of the visible back leg, adding a paw. Next draw in the tail.

Finish the drawing stage by adding the facial features: large eyes with double highlights, nose, mouth, and whiskers. Add ears, then a collar and bell.

Ink your sketch, defining the lines of the individual paws and of the end of the tail. Make the pupils black, and define the shading on the top of the head.

Color the cat ginger, leaving the lower face, paws, and end of the tail white. Finally, get some shading into the inner ears and onto the paws.

STRAY CAT STRUT

Here's another cat, this time in full strut along the top of a fence. The back curves up toward the tail, and his legs suggest a jaunty, lively gait. Note the happy expression on this kitty, who has her eyes closed in little arcs and eyebrows raised high. The white areas are typical cat markings, with white mask, paws, chest, belly, and tail tip.

Draw an ellipse for the head, adding triangles for the cheeks. Draw a circle for the rump and two curved lines for the body. Add a triangle for the back leg.

Work a straight line as an anchor, then add circles for the knee joints and paws with lines for the bones. Sit the paws on the line, then add a tail.

Add flesh to the four legs, and then flesh out the tail. Next, add two triangular ears.

Create the facial details: small slit eyes with tiny brows, nose, mouth, and whiskers. Then add a collar and bell. Finally, indicate panels in a fence.

Ink all the lines of the cat, including the individual paws.

Color the cat dark gray, leaving the end of the tail, lower half of the face, underbelly, and ends of the paws white.

GALLERY

lizard

right This animal is recognizably lizard-like, with typical large manga eyes, and exaggerated paws. The blue color and white spots add to the fantasy look.

chibi dog

above Chibi characters, including animals, are based on normal characters but exaggerated. Dogs are very popular pets in Japan, and adapt well to the chibi look.

is it a bird?

below With a duck-like beak, and overall penguin shape, this cute creature has a decidedly mammalian-looking tail.

chibi cat

above Having many characteristics of a domestic cat, such as the pointed ears and white paws and tip of the tail, this character is exaggeratedly cute, with its large eyes and tiny manga nose and mouth

mini dragon

below In some settings, this would be a ferocious creature, but it could also be a cute pet in the right story.

mouse

above A mouse can easily be stylized with big black eyes and a tiny smile. The tail on this character is supersize.

wild and woolly

below This is a great animal for a prehistoric tale, with touches of mammoth, sloth, and anteater. Highlighting and shade suggest the shagginess of the coat.

bear

left Some animals are hard to identify, but this doesn't really matter. Cuteness is what counts.

rodent

right Like the mouse, this stripy rodent creature has an exaggerated tail. The fantasy paws are almost dog-like.

ALLIGATOR

Not all animals are cute and cuddly, of course. The alligator here looks hungry enough to eat you!
As he's coming toward you, there is an element of foreshortening involved, so the head is large in
proportion to the body, and the tail snakes off up to the right of the drawing.

Start with a rounded triangular shape for the head, then add an ellipse for the body, Add two ovals for the joints and paws of the front legs, and lines for bones.

Add another oval behind the first one for the body, and add lines and ovals for the hind legs.

Flesh out the legs, and add the paws. Then draw in the double lines of the tail.

Draw the main features of the face: these are eyes on the top of the head, and the long snout. Create the curve of the mouth, filling it with spiky teeth.

Create the triangles of the ruff down the back and along the tail. Then indicate some scales on the back and legs.

Finally, add some shading, working along the back, inside the mouth, and down the legs. Add some shading around the eyes and get an indication of scales on the back.

TORTOISE

Another prehistoric-looking creature, but this one is much friendlier. This happy little tortoise is drawn in a more whimsical manga style, with a simple oval head and large, manga eyes. The legs are short and sturdy, and resemble an elephant's. Note that the pattern on the shell is created simply by shading.

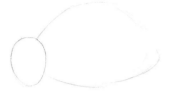

Start by drawing a circle for the head, then add an irregular ellipse for the body.

Add large ovals for the eyes, then draw the double line indicating where the neck sits in the shell. Draw a curved line for the bottom of the shell, then create the basic shape of the leg.

Draw the outline of highlights in the eyes, then shade the pupils. Add a mouth, then refine the profile of the shell. Indicate the three patches of scales on the paws on the legs.

Outline the scales on the back of the shell. Then suggest some shading on the legs.

Shade around and between the scales you indicated on the back, then add more shading on the legs, to improve their rounded profiles. Shade around the shell.

GREEN MONSTER

Of course, manga stories are also populated with imaginary animals of all shapes and sizes. This little green monster looks less than friendly, with his menacing eyes and sinister smirk. The single visible fang gives him a comical air though, and his body shape and proportions make him look laughably short.

Start by drawing a circle, then cut two semicircles into it. This gives you your basic body.

Now add four large sausage-shaped limbs.

Add eyes and a snout, with a line for the mouth. Add ears on the top of the head. Outline paw pads and indicate "fingers."

Ink over all your main lines, then ink in some indications of shading on the legs to improve their rounded profile.

Color your monster bright green, with a beige underbelly and beige paw pads. Use this color inside the ears too. Give him yellow eyes, leaving the fang white.

AQUATIC CREATURE

Here's another odd fellow, who looks like he probably lives under water, judging by the limbless body and frill of thin tentacles. He has a friendly, crumpled smile and appealing, round eyes, together with two little blue antennae on the top of his head. The white highlight gives a clear indication of the rounded shape of the creature.

Start by drawing a basic oval shape: this will serve as both head and body for this creature.

Add two circles for the eyes, then add a couple of tentacles with bobbly ends on top of the head.

Draw round pupils in the eyes, and give each eye a rounded highlight. Create a wavy mouth, then add a frond-like set of "legs" under the creature.

Use bright red for the body and frond-like legs, with ice blue for the tentacles and eyes. Finally get a white highlight onto the top of the head.

Ink the critter, including the wavy line of the mouth. Then, leaving the white highlight, ink the pupils black.

LONG-NECKED CREATURE

One of the fun things about making up imaginary creatures is using the features of existing animals and changing them round. This one has a long, giraffe-like neck, with a head like an anteater, stripes like a zebra, and a tail like a monkey. The little flutes on his head are expelling a puff of steam, and the short stubby legs mean he probably trots like a jaunty sausage-dog.

Draw an oval for the creature's body and a small oval for the head. Join them with a curved line for a long neck.

Flesh out the neck, giving it a curved profile. Then add four short legs underneath the body.

Next, add an eye and two flutes on the head, with a puff of steam coming out. Work a series of zigzag stripes down the back, and draw in a long straight tail ending in a curl. Finish with a long thin tongue curving out of the mouth.

Then ink all the main lines of your sketch and color the pupil black. Improve the lines of the toes. Then, ink over the zigzag lines using red ink.

Color the area you outlined in red ink using red, then color the rest of the creature honey beige. Use a darker shade on his neck and belly to round out his profile.

TREE DWELLER

This little character is clinging happily to some sort of tree trunk. His shape is koala-like, but he has a monkey-style face, and cute purple-and-yellow spotted markings. Note the two-toed feet and the way they are gripping the trunk, together with the three-fingered hands. The color may be for camouflage purposes, if he hides in trees with yellow and purple blossom.

Start by drawing a circle for the head, and a kidney bean shape for the body.

Next create circular joints for the shoulder and thigh. Add an indication of a tree trunk, then add fingers and toes to the limbs to hold the creature to the tree.

Add facial details: round eyes, with shaded pupils, a snub nose, and large smiling mouth. Then indicate circular detailing on the body. Add large ears.

Ink all the lines of your creature, and as you do so, add some contours to the tree. Color the pupils and snout black, leaving a white highlight.

Color the critter purple, giving him yellow patches. Color his face and the inside of the ears pale pink and gray.

KITTEN COUPLE

Even real animals can be given a fantasy twist with unusual coloring and cartoon faces. These two kitten-like creatures are colored in bright blue and lilac, and they have oversized manga eyes and simplified ears, paws, and tails. The way the rear one is standing upright makes him look a bit like a meerkat.

Start with two ovals for the heads then add basic body shapes, working on the relationship between the two kitty bodies.

Next add the visible legs, again looking at the relationship between the pair. Draw these as sausage shapes.

Now add the two long upright tails, one at each side of the composition. Then give both kitties two ears.

Draw in the large oval eyes, with large pupils and double highlights in each. Shade the pupils, then add noses, and whiskers, and paw lines.

Ink the main lines, establishing the pale area on the upright kitty. Ink the pupils, around the highlights. Finally, add some exclamation marks.

Color one of the kitties pale blue and the other pale lilac. Give them both pale honey eyes. Then add gray shadows under the bodies and on the faces.

LANDFISH

Here's another odd-looking hybrid. The body is that of a goldfish, but his forelegs are developed and he has prominent antennae and large lips. The rear limbs are flipper-like, and the tail is a bizarrely polka-dotted paddle shape. Note the gills running down the side of the body, and the white highlight which gives a shiny sheen to the skin.

Create the basic shape by drawing an oval on its side. Then add a tailfin to the back.

Place the two front legs with webbed feet, and add in the back feet: note that the second back foot consists only of the line of webbing.

Add the facial details: large eyes, with large pupils and treble highlights, then the thick, curved, rather feminine lips.

Then add curly antennae to the top of the head. Next add the curved lines of fins.

Ink the lines, and color the pupils and areas around the circle details using black. Establish the lines of the fins, the tentacles, and the facial details.

Leave white highlights above the fins, across into the top of the head, and around the rest of the mouth. Color all other parts of the creature a warm orange.

Weapons

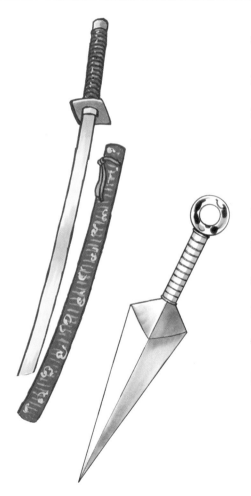

Weapons play a big part in action stories. As with other aspects of manga, many weapons are recognizable as real, but with elaboration or embellishments, while others are total fantasy or futuristic. Martial arts are common in manga stories, and weapons from these disciplines also appear often.

SHURIKEN THROWING STAR

Throwing stars like this are used by ninja warriors and martial arts fighters, and are sometimes known as hira shuriken. They are usually small enough to fit in the hand, and are held between the fingers in readiness for launching. Note how using shades of mauve-gray can give a good metallic sheen to your star.

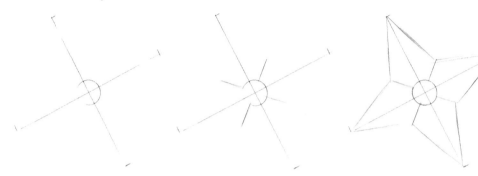

Start by drawing a circle, then cross it with two diagonal lines. Add a short line to the end of each, perpendicular to it.

Now add a short straight line from the circle out, in between the longer lines.

Then join the long and short lines to create a pointed star shape with the circle as its center.

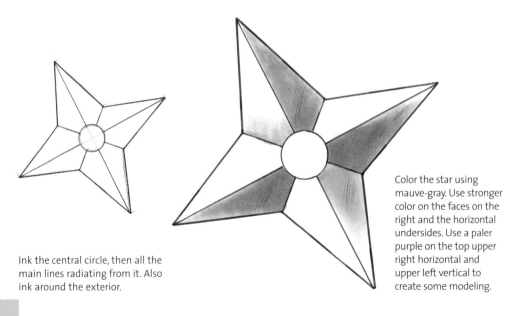

Ink the central circle, then all the main lines radiating from it. Also ink around the exterior.

Color the star using mauve-gray. Use stronger color on the faces on the right and the horizontal undersides. Use a paler purple on the top upper right horizontal and upper left vertical to create some modeling.

SHURIKEN THROWING DAGGER

These short daggers are also a throwing weapon, used in the same way as the star. They are small enough to sit between the fingers, and can be thrown in multiple volleys. Shuriken weapons are made in a variety of shapes. Note the grooved hilt, which helps the holder to keep a good grip, and the weighted end which gives balance to the throw.

Draw one circle inside another, with a straight line to indicate the centerline of a blade.

Add in the outline of the hilt, crossing it with a series of horizontal lines. Thicken the line of the end of the hilt.

Now add in the diamond-shaped top of the blade.

Using a ruler, create the lines of the blade, coming to a sharp point at the end.

Ink over the main lines of the end, hilt, and the blade. Add some black shading on the circular end.

Use a steely mauve to color the blade, making one half darker than the other to indicate shading. Add some shading to the right-hand side of the hilt.

KATANA SWORD

This is another common weapon in manga stories featuring samurai warriors. The katana is a traditional Japanese sword, dating back to the 1400s, and is still used for ceremonial purposes today. It consists of a long, curving blade and hilt, and was often used in tandem with a shorter version for close fighting.

Start by drawing two curved parallel lines.

At the end of them, construct a handle for the sword, with two crosspieces outlined.

Curve the profile of the end of the blade. Then indicate a crisscross design on the hilt.

Outline the profile of the blade, hilt, end, and crosspiece in ink, then ink the crisscross pattern on the hilt.

Color the hilt red and gray, with steely gray and white for the end and crosspiece. Finally use some pale gray on the blade to make it look shiny and metallic.

STAFF

A simple-looking staff like this can turn into a fearsome weapon in the hands of a master. Based on the traditional smaller three-section staff, or nunchaku, this heavyweight version can take out whole lines of opponents in a single sweep.

Draw a basic warrior figure in a martial stance. Give him two hands, and place a long stick created from parallel lines between them. Add a circular end.

Now create the detailing near the bottom end, and then repeat the shape at the top, and add similar detailing.

Ink the lines of the stick, the ends of the stick, and the details on the stick.

Add some initial shading onto the length of the stick, then gently shade the right-hand edges of the white tips to get some modeling here.

Working around the hands, color the stick black. Leave a highlight right down the center of the stick to help round it out. Finally, add gray highlights to the right of the white ends, again to help define their roundness.

FANTASY SWORD

In manga, you can let your imagination run wild, taking familiar objects and creating fantastic variants. This super-sized sword looks like it is completely unwieldy, but can be held by a single hand. The hilt is studded with jewels and is heavily decorated in gold. The blade itself is fearsome-looking, with a sharp cutaway section.

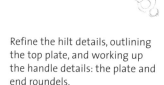

Start with a diagonal line, then bisect this with two lines perpendicular to it. Create a simple handle and a hand to clasp it, then indicate the top plate.

Refine the hilt details, outlining the top plate, and working up the handle details: the plate and end roundels.

Draw the curved blade, outlining it twice. Add details on the hilt end of the blade, here a triangle with circles, then add circle details to the broad plate.

Ink all the important details around the hilt and on the blade, and ink around the plates. Outline the double edge of the blade and the cutout. Add shading in ink.

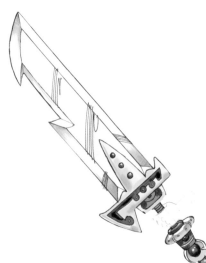

Use gold for the main areas of the hilt and plate, then use red to pick out the details. Leave white highlights that could be jewels or metallic details. Finally use an ice blue to create the metallic edges of the scimitar, and show where it is catching the light.

MAGIC SCEPTER

Another popular manga weapon is a magic-powered scepter. It is often used by female characters, and is a much less aggressive form of attack, utilizing bursts of light and flashes of crackling energy. The long handle can be highly ornamental and colorful, as seen in this example.

Begin by drawing an oval for the top of the weapon, then draw two verticals down to a point.

Starting at the top, add circular details. Define the line of the plate at the top. Add details halfway down, then add a couple of circular beads at the bottom.

Continue building up details on the stick. Then add some flowing ribbons hanging down from the top plate.

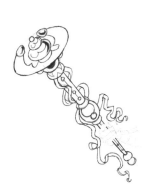

Use a fine pen to ink all the important lines, picking out details on all the various decorative elements. Outline the flowing ribbons.

Color the handle red, with red details for the bobbles. Add yellow and pale red ribbons. Finally create a yellow burst around the top of the weapon.

ARM PLASMA CANNON

Manga characters can be equipped with all kinds of electronic and technological weaponry. The basic rule is detailing—with mechanical hardware, the more the merrier! An arm-mounted cannon like this one, for instance, has a variety of shapes and features. It sits snugly around the forearm, with a high hand grip for stability and a low-slung nozzle for firing plasma bolts. The ammunition is fed through to the main weapon body from super-insulated tubing behind.

Create an arm from basic shapes for joints and lines for bones, then flesh it out and add a basic hand. Add a torso.

Now begin to sketch some rough shapes for a handle, and a rectangular block around the forearm, with further blocks underneath the arm.

Work in lots of details to give your drawing a mechanical look. Try and imagine the possible purpose of the pieces you add to make them more convincing. Add a suggestion of a nozzle, switches and controls, and a coiling tube behind the body.

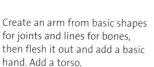

Finally, color your drawing using shades of gray and mauve. Define the light source from above, with darker tones of gray on the underside of the weapon, and leave lighter highlights on the handle and tubing.

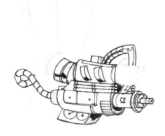 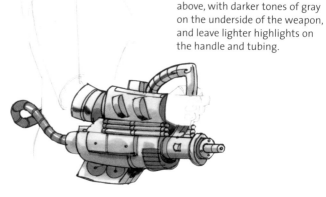

Next, ink your drawing, including some solid blacks to suggest shadows, and to give a metallic sheen to the cylindrical handle and arm support. Use a finer pen to ink the details such as the grooves on the tubing and on the handle.

HAND BLASTER

A compact hand blaster is a good personal weapon in a manga tale of the future. This solid-looking example is composed of simple shapes, based on a contemporary handgun. The handle, or grip, should be shaped to fit comfortably in the hand, with a trigger positioned where it meets the barrel.

 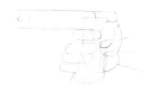 

Start by drawing a gripping hand shape, with the index finger slightly separated, then sketch in the shape of the handle in a curving rectangle.

Draw a cylindrical barrel with two circles at its end, then work the other end of the barrel. Add detailing around the barrel.

Add the trigger and trigger guard, then build up the detail on the barrel and stock, and add a magazine chamber jutting down from the barrel in front of the trigger.

Ink all the main lines of your drawing and when the ink is dry, erase any pencil marks.

Color your weapon with dark grays for a solid, metallic look. Use a darker shade for the grip and detailing, and use some white highlights on top of the barrel to give added depth.

FINGER LASERS

For a more subtle and personal touch, your character could use these fingertip-mounted laser blasters. Each blaster sits snugly over the first joint of the finger, and is made of from polished steel. Note the position of the hand for firing, and the soft blue light emanating from all the laser beams.

  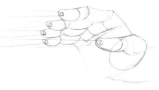

Draw a basic hand shape from lines and circles for joints, then define the joints as more rectangular. Make the thumb read as separate.

Add circles to the ends of the fingers and thumb. Then define the joints more closely and sharpen the profile of the palm.

Now lightly indicate the laser beams coming from the nozzles on each fingertip.

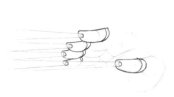 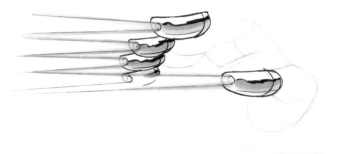

Ink the joints of the thumb, then ink the other finger joints.

Create rounded profiles using white, black, and gray, with touches of blue. Then color the lasers using pale blue.

ASSAULT RIFLE

A sturdier field weapon could be this solid assault rifle, with shoulder strap and telescopic sight. The rifle has a grip, a stock, and a magazine chamber at the front, and the overall shape is bulky and heavy, to emphasize the idea of a powerful piece of hardware.

Start with three basic shapes, for the barrel, grip, and magazine.

Add a cylinder shape to the end of the barrel, with a thinner muzzle and sight, then draw a stock on the rear, pointing diagonally down.

Build up the detail on the barrel, adding a telescopic sight and a trigger, with molding on the grip and magazine.

Finish the drawing with a snaking shoulder strap.

Ink the drawing, including all the fine details.

Lastly, color the rifle with purples and grays, adding white highlights to the top areas, then use darker gray to color the molding below.

GALLERY

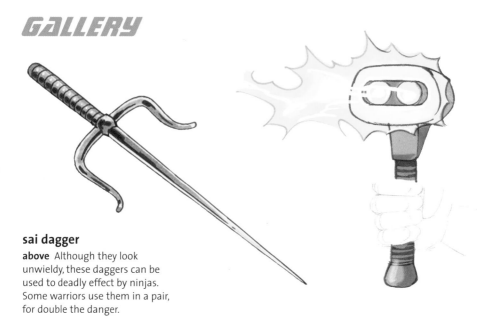

sai dagger

above Although they look unwieldy, these daggers can be used to deadly effect by ninjas. Some warriors use them in a pair, for double the danger.

blaster

above Blasting from dual "barrels" this adds color and drama to a scene.

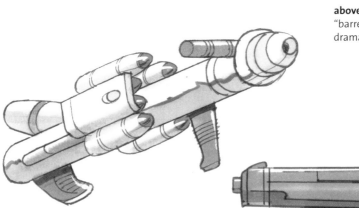

rapid fire

above With features reminiscent of a spaceship, this futuristic weapon would work for any space warrior.

handgun

right This model is based on a standard handgun with stock, trigger, and barrel. It is suitable for many storylines.

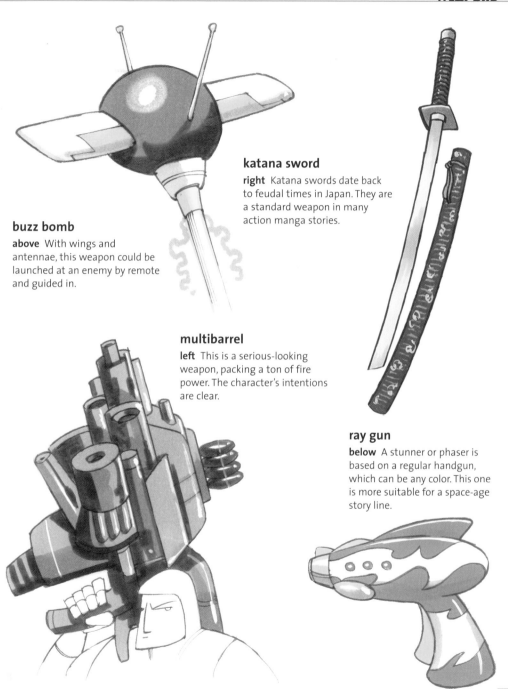

katana sword

right Katana swords date back to feudal times in Japan. They are a standard weapon in many action manga stories.

buzz bomb

above With wings and antennae, this weapon could be launched at an enemy by remote and guided in.

multibarrel

left This is a serious-looking weapon, packing a ton of fire power. The character's intentions are clear.

ray gun

below A stunner or phaser is based on a regular handgun, which can be any color. This one is more suitable for a space-age story line.

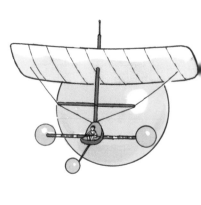

Vehicles

You can really let your imagination go wild when it comes to vehicles. You can start with something that is real, such as a car or plane, and then customize it as you see fit. If your stories feature space travel and futuristic scenes, there is no limit to what you can draw. Practice these examples to get yourself going.

MOBILE PATROL BATTLE ARMOR

Fighting armor and battle suits feature in many sci-fi manga stories. Here is an idea for a patrol vehicle, equipped with sensors, cameras, and cannon lasers. The jointed legs can extend to full height to give extra width of vision. The hands comprise three fast-rotating impact blasters for a scatter-gun attack. The pilot sits in the egg-shaped capsule at the top, with twin visibility apertures.

Start by drawing two torpedo shapes, one on top of the other.

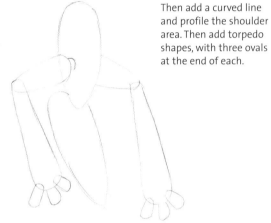

Then add a curved line and profile the shoulder area. Then add torpedo shapes, with three ovals at the end of each.

From the left-hand oval, create an upcurving joint and a downward point of attachment for two round wheels.

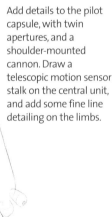

Add details to the pilot capsule, with twin apertures, and a shoulder-mounted cannon. Draw a telescopic motion sensor stalk on the central unit, and add some fine line detailing on the limbs.

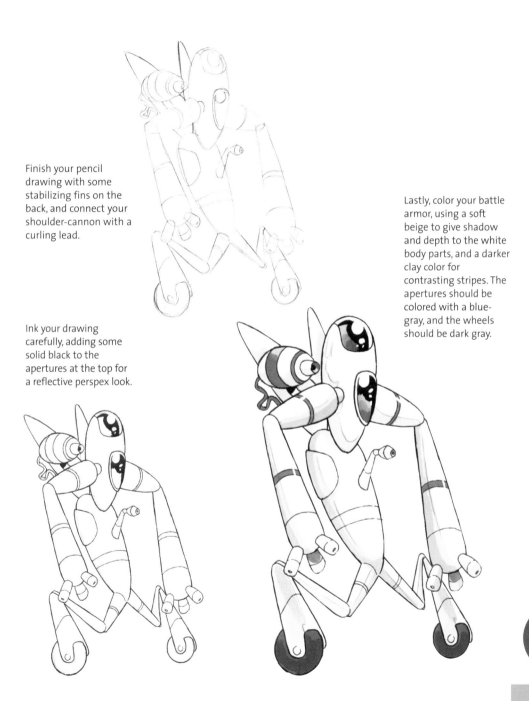

Finish your pencil drawing with some stabilizing fins on the back, and connect your shoulder-cannon with a curling lead.

Lastly, color your battle armor, using a soft beige to give shadow and depth to the white body parts, and a darker clay color for contrasting stripes. The apertures should be colored with a blue-gray, and the wheels should be dark gray.

Ink your drawing carefully, adding some solid black to the apertures at the top for a reflective perspex look.

HIGH-SPEED APPREHENSION UNIT

This is a fast, agile unit for high-speed pursuit. Its low, wide shape gives extra stability in a chase, and its flat, squat wheels are excellent for all terrain. The front of the vehicle is equipped with high-velocity static-shock cannons, which can disable the electronic systems of a fleeing vehicle at a distance of three miles. The shielding canopy is designed to withstand aerial bombardment and doubles up as a solar panel for extra fuel efficiency.

Start by drawing a rectangle, then create a curved front.

Next outline a wheel at each corner, using basic shapes. Make the wheels at the front smaller than those at the back.

Add detail for the passenger well and roof. Then on the near underside create engineering details. Add a shield canopy to the top.

Finish your drawing by adding two static-shock cannons on the front of the unit.

Ink the lines of your car. The inking can be very simple, except for the engine detailing under the car.

Color the wheels in shades of dark gray to show their roundness. Make the body of the car red, with a white stripe and a white shield on top. Keep the cannons white, and use a shade of beige to suggest shape.

RIOT BUSTER

This is a vehicle designed for breaking up public disturbances in confined urban streets. It is compact and built for single-operator use. The spiked battering ram at the front will quickly clear a path through an unruly mob, and the twin rocket launchers either side of the cab can unleash multiple volleys of resin pellets, which are non-fatal but very effective. The rear 'exhaust' pipes are for spraying tear gas over a wide area.

Start with a large oval, and a small circle cutting at the bottom left.

Draw the battering ram around the front circle, and add a curving rectangle for a door.

Behind the door, add a large wheel, and a smaller stabilizing wheel at the rear. Draw two rocket launchers, one on either side of the unit.

Next, add spikes to the battering ram, and four exhaust pipes protruding from the rear. Draw in some headlights, and indicate the curve of a seat in the cabin.

Ink all the main lines of your drawing, and give a chrome look to the exhaust by using a wavy solid black line. A brush pen is good for this.

Color using a dull mauve-gray for the body, with a darker gray for the wheels and a cream for the internal upholstery. Add a little yellow to the headlights.

TROOP-DISPERSAL CARRIER

This is an aerial troop-carrier which can transport huge armies across long distances. The curving teardrop shape gives the impression of a menacing insect in flight, creating a sense of unease in any opposing forces. The carrier is driven by two giant propeller engines, and underneath is the dispersal pod for unloading. On the top of the fuselage is a control and observation deck.

Start with a large semi-elliptical shape, with a shallow semicircle underneath.

Add two ellipses to the top of the vehicle. These lines define the vehicle as a plane and form its cabin, wings, and fuselage.

Work up some detail, adding in the cockpit and two propellers.

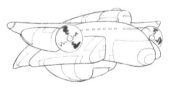

Indicate windows in the cabin, and redefine the nose cone. Add the light to the upper carriage.

Ink all the main lines, to show the detailing in the cabin and fuselage where sheets have been joined. Outline the windows, then use black to create the whirring motion of the propellers.

Color the vehicle using sand. Color the nose cone, the center of the propellers, and the tail fin gold, with red for the light.

EXPLORATORY CONVOY TRAIN

This is a vehicle widely used during mankind's expansion into outer space. It can cope with all kinds of hostile atmospheres, and its super-thick shell is designed to cope with a wide range of gravitational pressures. The train can carry all the necessary building tools and supplies needed to sustain a human colony for several years, and can carry up to a thousand individuals. The giant caterpillar tracks are flexible enough to cope with unpredictable terrain.

Start with a two-point perspective block, with a line going off onto the horizon.

Use these perspective lines to help you create a series of carriages. The grow smaller as they recede into the distance.

On the front of the train, draw a large caterpillar tread and add some rectangular blocks on either side of the carriages.

Next, draw the blasters on the far side of the lead carriage. Add some grooves for windows, some wheels, and indicate an elevator boarding tube on the right, with some small figures to show scale.

Ink your drawing carefully, using some small lines to indicate texture on the train and also on the ground.

Finally, color with dull gray-beige, and charcoal gray for the caterpillar tracks. Use a little sand color for the ground, and add some cool gray shadows around the blasters.

MOBILE ENVIRONMENT

Other worlds may be unable to sustain human life. This mobile, self-contained habitat can be used to explore while enabling the population to live a reasonably normal existence. The main dome contains a large-sized natural environment, with fields, trees, mountains, and rivers, and can accommodate a city-sized population. The smaller, secondary dome contains a miniature sea. The whole environment travels on a series of omni-directional spherical wheels.

Draw a vertical center line, then create a low oval out to each side.

Using the center line, add a dome over the top of the profile.

Draw in a central apron to ground level, then on either side add a series of wheels. Add some trunking on the apron.

Sketch in some mountains, trees, and hills in the main dome, and an indication of water in the small one.

Ink your drawing, indicating some reflective spots on the dome, and some solid blacks between the wheels.

Color your drawing, using gray for the vehicle base, and blues, mauves, and greens for the natural environment.

CRUISE SHIP

This craft is built to take large numbers of people on pleasure cruises around the polluted oceans of a future earth. The seawater is toxic, so the ship has to be completely enclosed and sit high up out of the water to avoid contamination of any passengers. It is driven by two side-mounted jet engines, which churn through the stagnant waters. On the left toward the rear is the viewing cabin, which is the nearest the passengers can safely get to the sea.

Create a curved irregular polygon, and lightly indicate a water line.

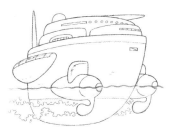

Add details of a cabin on the deck, together with some portholes for passengers to gather behind.

Now add two large jet-propulsion engines on either side, and indicate the churning water in their wake.

Draw a viewing cabin at the rear, and add portholes and a forward antenna at the top.

Ink your drawing, including all the portholes and the wake behind the propulsion units.

Color the main body of the ship yellow, with white upper cabins and viewing cabin. Use gray for some shading, and color the sea with a dirty-looking gray blue, light enough so that you can still see the bottom of the ship.

GALLERY

battle suit

left This vehicle is based on a humanoid shape. Contrasting colors give it impact, while a touch of black on the main surfaces makes them look like reflective plastic.

spiked bike

above Part-weapon, part-vehicle, this craft has spikes that could destroy a pursuing vehicle without any trouble: it shreds tires, tracks, and anything else that gets in the way.

superbike

below There is no sign of any weapons on this three-wheeled bike with a dark, sinister rider— but there's no hitching a ride either. Speed lines give the bike some motion.

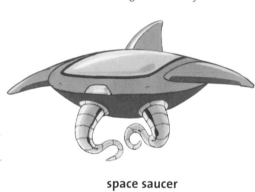

space saucer

above A vehicle like this one can fly, possibly even in space. It looks slightly menacing, with its dangling tentacles, curved wings, and green color.

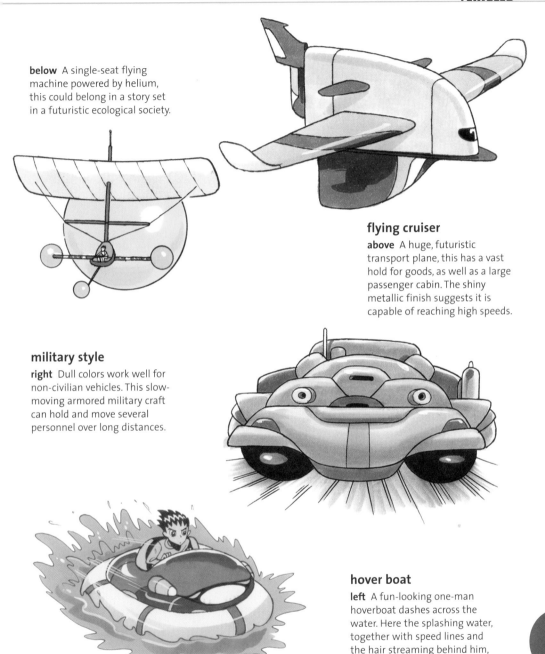

below A single-seat flying machine powered by helium, this could belong in a story set in a futuristic ecological society.

flying cruiser

above A huge, futuristic transport plane, this has a vast hold for goods, as well as a large passenger cabin. The shiny metallic finish suggests it is capable of reaching high speeds.

military style

right Dull colors work well for non-civilian vehicles. This slow-moving armored military craft can hold and move several personnel over long distances.

hover boat

left A fun-looking one-man hoverboat dashes across the water. Here the splashing water, together with speed lines and the hair streaming behind him, combine to give a sense of speed.

INDEX

Authors acknowledgments
Thanks to all the talented writers, artists, colorists,
letterers and editors who make comics such a
wonderful world. While working on this book I was
listening to Transystem V and Theoretical Girl.